PRAISE FOR *THE WAY UNDER THE WAY*

"When I read Mark Nepo's luminous, meditative poems, one word stands tall in the mind and silence that follows—BEFRIEND. He does not avert his eyes from the difficult moment or the lost hour. He stays steady to feel the magnificence again. And somehow, organically and instinctively, he is able to pass that hopeful calm on to us in ways we desperately need, these and all days."

NAOMI SHIHAB NYE
author of *Words Under the Words*

"In this magical book, Mark Nepo ushers us to the depth of who we are and where we truly live. His words, like pearls for the human soul, awaken us. Give yourself the gift of this treasured book and let it touch the depths of your heart with its richness."

AGAPI STASSINOPOULOS
author of *Unbinding the Heart*

"Mark Nepo's poems are like rare wine that directly nourishes the soul. These are stories of the heart, of brokenness that heals, of grief that awakens us to joy. They remind us of what is essential and sacred, of what we share in the depths of our humanity. Rather than offering answers, they open our questions to the greater mystery of what it means to be alive, to feel. His words welcome us to witness the wonder of who we really are."

LLEWELLYN VAUGHAN-LEE, PHD
Sufi teacher and author

PRAISE FOR MARK NEPO

"Mark Nepo has a great heart. His poems are good company."
COLEMAN BARKS
translator of *The Essential Rumi*

"Mark Nepo joins a long tradition of truth-seeking, wild-hearted poets—Rumi, Walt Whitman, Emily Dickinson, Mary Oliver—and deserves a place in the center of the circle with them."
ELIZABETH LESSER
cofounder, Omega Institute,
author of *Broken Open* and *Marrow*

"Mark Nepo has a rare quality of writing, one that fills you up even as it drops you into emptiness. Through his sensibilities we touch what is human: he plucks at our heartstrings with naked candor and metaphorical mastery."
JULIE CLAYTON
New Consciousness Review

"Mark Nepo is one of the finest spiritual guides of our time."
PARKER J. PALMER
author of *A Hidden Wholeness* and *The Courage to Teach*

"Nepo is a consummate storyteller with a rare gift for making the invisible visible."
PUBLISHERS WEEKLY

"Mark Nepo is a rare being, a poet who does not overuse language, a wise man without arrogance, a teacher who always speaks with compassion, and an easygoing love-to-listen-to-him storyteller."
JAMES FADIMAN, PHD
cofounder, Institute for Transpersonal Psychology

THE WAY
UNDER
THE WAY

ALSO BY MARK NEPO

NONFICTION
The One Life We're Given
The Endless Practice
Seven Thousand Ways to Listen
Finding Inner Courage
Unlearning Back to God
The Exquisite Risk
The Book of Awakening

FICTION
As Far As the Heart Can See

POETRY
Inside the Miracle
Reduced to Joy
Surviving Has Made Me Crazy
Suite for the Living
Inhabiting Wonder
Acre of Light
Fire Without Witness
God, the Maker of the Bed, and the Painter

EDITOR
Deepening the American Dream

RECORDINGS
The One Life We're Given
Inside the Miracle (expanded edition, 2015)
Reduced to Joy
The Endless Practice
Seven Thousand Ways to Listen
Staying Awake
Holding Nothing Back
As Far As the Heart Can See
The Book of Awakening
Finding Inner Courage
Finding Our Way in the World
Inside the Miracle (1996)

THE WAY UNDER THE WAY

The Place of True Meeting

MARK NEPO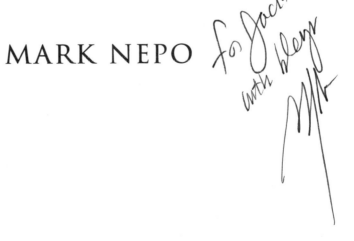

SOUNDS TRUE
BOULDER, COLORADO

Sounds True
Boulder, CO 80306

Sounds True is a trademark of Sounds True, Inc.

Published 2016

Cover design by Jennifer Miles
Book design by Beth Skelley

Printed in Canada

Library of Congress Cataloging-in-Publication Data
Names: Nepo, Mark, author.
Title: The way under the way : the place of true meeting, three books of poems /
    Mark Nepo.
Description: Boulder, CO : Sounds True, 2016.
Identifiers: LCCN 2016020373 (print) | LCCN 2016026490 (ebook) |
    ISBN 9781622037544 (hardcover : alk. paper) | ISBN 9781622037544 (ebook)
Classification: LCC PS3564.E6 A6 2016 (print) | LCC PS3564.E6 (ebook) |
    DDC 811/.54—dc23
LC record available at https://lccn.loc.gov/2016020373

10 9 8 7 6 5 4 3 2 1

I confess, the thousand poems I've written
and the books of philosophy have all
been threads pulled to a Source.

Like one who climbs a steep ravine
for fear of being trapped at the bottom,
I have lost my way into the open.

How could I know you were climbing
on the other side.

CONTENTS

FIRE IN THE TEMPLE

THE GREAT OPENING

LETTING WHAT IS SHINE

IN

SOFTER THAN TRUTH

A Thousand Stories On

The End of All Striving

In Conversation with Life

I began writing poetry when my first love moved on. I was nineteen and my heart was broken. I didn't have any true friends yet and so I began talking to myself, by writing. In time, I began to mend and realized that through my raw and honest reflection I'd begun a lifelong conversation with the Universe. This is the medicine of poetry: that through raw and honest reflection, we deepen our conversation with life. The purpose of poetry and expression is to make life real, to remove everything that gets in the way, and to help us live.

For me, the poems arrive with their wisdom. I retrieve them, more than create them, and they become my teachers. What they have to say becomes my inner curriculum and, by staying in conversation with the poems, I learn and grow. Whether you write or not, this way of learning is available to us all, as we meet and learn from the moments of our lives. Whether familiar with poetry or not, I invite you to receive these poems as you would a friend who's eager to share intimately. Let the feeling reach you first. For the power of a poem is how it awakens your own feeling.

The longer I live, the more the life of poetry and the poetry of life blur. Early on, I wanted to write great poems, but when brought to my knees by cancer in my thirties, I needed to discover true poems to help me live. Now, in my sixties, I want to be the poem. After all these years, I've learned that, in the deepest sense, poetry is a way of engaging the world with our being and care. And more than understanding whatever a poet might mean in any given poem, the poetry is there to ignite your own exploration of aliveness.

So I want to thank you for opening this book, for pausing in the making of our modern hive long enough to explore the nature and workings of the inner life. The inner life is essential because we can grow hypnotized by a world that keeps building monuments to itself. Beforehand, our want to build can seem like a great dream of the future, and the intoxication of building itself can seem like a marvel of progress. But often, once built, the overgrowth of all we make can spread like the metastasis of an idea only concerned with its self-replication. There is nothing wrong with dreaming and building, but the dangers arise once we're overgrown.

Ultimately, our devotion to the foundation of things is imperative because without our foundations, we would be buried under the collapse of our own constructions, both personally and globally. Without healthy roots, the forest would fall. And poetry is the study and care of roots—human roots, ontological roots, mystical roots, and the lineage of roots.

In this regard, the human experiment has always needed poets, philosophers, prophets, and social visionaries to point to the ways that we overgrow the simple miracle of life, to keep alive the ways we can self-diagnose our obsessions and excesses, and to encourage our self-repair and renewal.

As we begin, I ask that you listen to these poems with the angel sleeping in your heart, the one we carry around in case of emergency, in case the gift of life is suddenly revealed as precious enough that we should wake the red angel *now*—desperate for it to bring us alive in the deepest terms possible.

THREE IN THE NEST

This collection contains three separate books of poetry. Together, they include 217 poems retrieved and shaped over the past twenty years. It's been humbling to put them together, and to watch them grow, and most of all, to learn from them. We're all drawn to what we need to learn, which if engaged with an open heart reveals insights common to us all.

The first two books in this collection, *Suite for the Living* and *Inhabiting Wonder*, were originally published by Bread for the Journey in 2004 because of the wholehearted support of Wayne Muller and Marianna Cacciatore. I'm grateful for how they've shared and read my poems in public for years. These two books bear witness to the messy and magnificent journey of being human, infused as it is with our irrepressible kindness and resilience.

The original books were wonderfully received and sold out of their first editions. Wherever I speak and teach, people kindly ask for them. It's a joy to bring them back into print as part of this volume. It's also almost impossible for a poet not to evolve a book further. And so, I've integrated twenty-six new poems into *Suite for the Living* and thirty-two new poems into *Inhabiting Wonder*.

The third book in this collection, *The Way Under the Way*, gathers eighty-three of my most recent poems. It centers on the place of true meeting that is always near, where we chance to discover our shared humanity and common thread of Spirit.

Looking back, the life of these poems reveals a shift of being that has unfolded between trouble and wonder. I offer them as aids in living, listening, and beholding what matters. I offer them as small wonders found and cared for through the years. I ask you to walk with them in case one or two might help us find each other, so we can say that all of what's before us is more than enough. I hope you might be drawn to one that, held close to your heart, will serve as a guide.

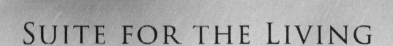

BOOK ONE

SUITE FOR THE LIVING

for Susan and Robert,
whose spirits
let me see
my hands
in the dark

THE NECESSARY ART

Poetry is the unexpected utterance of the soul that comes to renew us when we least expect it. More than the manipulation of language, it is a necessary art by which we live and breathe. It is the art of embodied perception; a braiding of heart and mind around experience. Consider how a simple fish inhales water, and somehow, mysteriously and miraculously, it extracts the oxygen from the water. In doing this, it turns that water into the air by which it breathes. This ongoing inner transformation is poetry. A much deeper process than fooling with words. For us, the heart is our gill and we must move forward into life, like simple fish, or we will die. And the mysterious yet vital way we turn experience into air, the way we extract what keeps us alive—this is the poetry of life that transcends any earthly endeavor. All this while the Universal Ground of Being we call Spirit is working its unknowable physics on us, eroding us to know that we are each other.

As sheet music is meant to be played, poetry is meant to be felt and heard. In this way, what we feel in our depths is poetry waiting to be voiced. And just as music, once heard, stirs our very being, voicing our feelings stirs our consciousness. So I encourage you to take the time to read aloud the poems that touch you, so they and you can come alive. After all these years, I can affirm that the gift of poetry is how it allows us to be intimate with all things.

The assumption of all poetry is that when we're connected, each of us is able to be more fully alive. Poetry finds and gives voice to those connections. But as we keep trying to inhabit the possibilities we carry within, we're inevitably stopped by the fires of experience that burn down the temples we have built, whether it be the temple of our dreams or the temple of our love or the sanctuary of our secret ambitions. Like it or not, the fire of experience is a stripping away—a stripping down of the ways we feel compelled to please or meet the expectations of others, a breaking down of the demands that tell us who and how we should love. Until the soul sheds what holds it back. Until we look to Spirit and Nature to teach us how to live. This undoing is necessary because it's breaking surface through our pain and sorrow that liberates us. It's coming alive again in the same life that releases beauty in the world.

There are a thousand ways to break surface, a thousand ways to survive the burning of temples, a thousand ways to raise our heavy hearts so we might be surprised by the release of our inner beauty, and a thousand ways to enter the great opening that follows heartache and loss. These poems explore some of those ways.

The sections in the first book in this collection explore how initiation and experience open us to the depth of life. In the section "Breaking Surface," the poems affirm the many ways that we break ground into authenticity. In the section "Fire in the Temple," the poems uncover the ways that life, often against our will, makes us bring what's inside out. And in the section "The Great Opening," the poems explore the unexpected vastness that honest living leads us to.

A word about the title sequence, "Suite for the Living," which is comprised of six smaller poems that appear as the last section. Each was written at the crest of a troubled time, just before I broke surface in yet another way. The six poems appeared over a period of eighteen years. Each felt complete unto itself at the time, and each served as a guide for the phase of life I was moving through. It was only after living with them for all those years that I realized—they belong together.

Like beads for a necklace I didn't know they would form, I worked to polish each—only to discover, beyond any conscious knowing or intent, that these expressions were a suite of poems. They were revealed to me slowly, the way the insights of our lives appear, forming one by one. Over time, the beads of wisdom we earn reveal their power as we discover that they and we and everything living belong to each other.

BREAKING SURFACE

You didn't come into this house so I might tear off
a piece of your life. Perhaps when you leave
you'll take something of mine: chestnuts,
roses or a surety of roots. . . .
PABLO NERUDA

BREAKING SURFACE

Let no one keep you from your journey,
no rabbi or priest, no mother
who wants you to dig for treasures
she misplaced, no father
who won't let one life be enough,
no lover who measures their worth
by what you might give up,
no voice that tells you in the night
it can't be done.

Let nothing dissuade you
from seeing what you see
or feeling the winds that make you
want to dance alone
or go where no one
has yet to go.

You are the only explorer.
Your heart, the unreadable compass.
Your soul, the shore of a promise
too great to be ignored.

WHERE NO ONE
STAYS A STATUE

It was a sunny day
and I went to the park
and sat on a bench. I was
one of many coming out
from under our rocks
to warm and lengthen.

He was two benches down,
a gentle older man
staring off into the place
between things, beyond
any simple past, staring
into the beginning or the end,
it was hard to say.

When he came up
our eyes met
and he knew I'd seen him
journey there and back.

There was no point in looking away.
And so, he shuffled over
and sat beside me. The sun
moved behind the one cloud
and he finally said
in half a quiver, "How
can we go there together?"

I searched my small mind
for an answer. At this,
he looked away and the sun came out
and I realized this is what the lonely
sages of China were talking about,
what the moon has whispered
before turning full for centuries,
what dancers leap for, what violinists
dream after fevering their last note.

But I was awkward and unsure.
He stared, as if to search my will,
and after several minutes,
he just patted my knee
and left.

I watched him
darken and brighten in the sun,
and vowed to look
in the folds of every cry
for a way through,
and hope someday
to meet him there.

THE LESSON

When young, it was the first fall from love.
It broke me open the way lightning splits a tree.
Then, years later, cancer broke me further.
This time, it broke me wider the way a flood
carves the banks of a narrow stream.
Then, having to leave a twenty-year marriage.
This broke me the way wind shatters glass.
Then, in Africa, it was the anonymous face
of a schoolboy beginning his life.
This broke me yet again. But this
was like hot water melting soap.

Each time I tried to close
what had been opened.
It was a reflex, natural enough.
But the lesson was, of course, the other way—
in never closing again.

In Muir Woods

Masters of stillness,
masters of light,
who, when cut by something
falling, go nowhere and heal,
teach me this nowhere,

who, when falling themselves,
simply wait to root
in another direction,
teach me this falling.

Four-hundred-year-old trees,
who draw aliveness from the Earth
like smoke from the heart of God,
we come, not knowing
you will hush our little want
to be big;

we come, not knowing
that all the work is so much
busyness of mind; all
the worry, so much
busyness of heart.

As the sun warms anything near,
being warms everything still,
and the great still things
that outlast us

make us crack
like leaves of laurel
releasing a fragrance
that has always been.

CROSSING SOME OCEAN
IN MYSELF

Half a century, and finally,
what I feel is what I say and
what I say is what I mean.

What I mean is that others, so used
to my gargantuan efforts to be good,
don't understand my efforts to be real.
They find me coming up short.

I'm simply burning old masks.
And the next step takes me—
I don't know where—
as it should be—
I don't know—
just that I love who I love.
I listen with my heart.
I struggle with the reflexes of my mind.

I mean, the pains of life are sharper now
but disappear more clearly the way
knives are swallowed by the sea.
And the subtleties of being come on
like waves that cleanse but which,
when dry, I can't seem to find.

So much like a gentle animal now,
unsure what I was fighting for,
except to breathe and sing, except

to call out the human names for God
that others have uttered when
hurt and confused.

So much like a love animal now
until the end of any day's work
is the soft moment
when loving and being loved
are the same.

And all year round,
the birds and trees instruct,
make visible the wind
the way reaching without shame
makes visible the love.

FIGHTING THE INSTRUMENT

Often the instruments of change
are not kind or just
and the hardest openness
of all might be
to embrace the change
while not wasting your heart
fighting the instrument.

The storm is not as important
as the path it opens.
The mistreatment in one life
never as crucial as the clearing
it makes in your heart.

This is very difficult to accept.
The hammer or cruel one
is always short-lived
compared to the jewel
in the center of the stone.

THE MUSIC BENEATH THE MUSIC

I have tried so hard to please
that I never realized
no one is watching.

I imagined like everyone at school
that our parents were sitting
just out of view like those
quiet doctors behind clean mirrors.

I even felt the future
gather like an audience,
ready to marvel at how much
we had done with so little.

But when I woke bleeding after surgery
with all those mothlike angels
breathing against me, I couldn't
talk and the audience was gone.

I cried way inside and the sobs
were no more than the water
of a deshelled spirit
soaking ground.

Years have passed and I wait
long hours in the sun to see the birch
fall of its own weight into the lake
and it seems to punctuate God's mime.

Nothing sad about it.

And sometimes, at night,
when the dog is asleep
and the owl is beginning to stare
into what no one ever sees,
I stand on the deck and feel
the black spill off the stars,
feel it coat the earth, the trees,
the minds of children half-asleep,
feel the stillness evaporate
all notions of fame
into the space
that waits
for light.

Unearthed Again

It starts out simple,
gets complicated and, by
burning what is not real,
gets simple again.

But it's never done.
No matter if we're tired,
spring comes and some undying
impulse breaks ground.

It's the same with denial. Or pain.
Or love. One day, if blessed, the tulip
coated with soil is again a tulip,
and with an urgency we thought
we left behind,
we must wake.

I think we could forget
all the ways to study in school
and just wait for this moment.

Those who wake are the students.
Those who stay awake are the teachers.

How we take turns.

ACCEPTING THIS

Yes, it is true. I confess,
I have thought great thoughts,
and sung great songs—all of it
rehearsal for the majesty
of being held.

The dream is awakened
when thinking I love you
and life begins
when saying I love you
and joy moves like blood
when embracing others with love.

My efforts now turn
from trying to outrun suffering
to accepting love wherever
I can find it.

Stripped of causes and plans
and things to strive for,
I have discovered everything
I could need or ask for
is right here—
in flawed abundance.

We cannot eliminate hunger,
but we can feed each other.
We cannot eliminate loneliness,
but we can hold each other.

We cannot eliminate pain,
but we can live a life
of compassion.

Ultimately,
we are small living things
awakened in the stream,
not gods who carve out rivers.

Like human fish,
we're asked to experience
meaning in the life that moves
through the gill of our heart.

There is nothing to do
and nowhere to go.
Accepting this,
we can do everything
and go anywhere.

WALKING NORTH

No matter how I turn
the magnificent light follows.
Background to my sadness.

No matter how I lift my heart
my shadow creeps in wait behind.
Background to my joy.

No matter how fast I run
a stillness without thought is where I end.

No matter how long I sit
there's a river of motion I must rejoin.

And when I can't hold my head up
it always falls in the lap of one
who has just opened.

When I finally free myself of burden
there's always someone's heavy head
landing in my arms.

The reasons of the heart
are leaves in wind.
Stand up tall and everything
will nest in you.

We all lose and we all gain.
Dark crowds the light.
Light fills the pain.

It's a conversation with no end,
a dance with no steps,
a song with no words,
a reason too big for any mind.

No matter how I turn
the magnificence follows.

AT STADIUM AND DRAKE

I was waiting to make a left, to get out
of traffic. She was across from me, in a
red hatchback, waiting to enter. The cars
whizzed by like hornets. Our eyes met briefly
and the whole journey was suddenly evident:
always going somewhere, always unsure how
to get there, waiting for the chance to join,
to lead, to follow, relieved to make our way,
till we miss our exit and wonder, "Where to
now?" The speed of the traffic made our cars
shimmy. We caught each other's eye again,
missing our chance. She shrugged. I laughed.
The moment of pause had opened a different
dimension that made us impervious to the pull
of the hive, at least for a while. Then, in a flash,
she was sucked into the whir. Someone behind
me began honking. I couldn't move. I wanted
out. Once home, I had a glass of water on the
deck, where the peony, weighed down with
all its beauty, was drinking from the birdbath.
I thought, "Oh, teach me how to stop."

THE FIRE THAT
TAKES NO WOOD

As a boy, I woke near a center
I couldn't name and every time
I ventured out, I was cut or hit
and thrown back in.

As a man, I find life to be a
meeting of centers and it's the
crossing from center to center
that suffers our clumsiness. It's
the crossing from what I alone
experience to what you alone
experience that sets fires in
the world. But once aflame,
we are humbly the same.

No one ever told me that
as snakes shed skin, as trees
snap bark, the human breast
peels, crying when forced open,
singing when loved open.

And whatever keeps us
from burning truth as food,
whatever tricks the heart into
thinking we can hide in the open,
whatever makes us look everywhere
but in our core—this is the smoke
that drives us from the living.

And whatever keeps us coming
back, coming up, whatever makes
us build a home out of straw, out
of heartache, out of nothing, what-
ever ignites us to see again for the
very first time—this is the bluish
flame that keeps the Earth
grinding to the sun.

LOOK AROUND

If you try to comprehend air
before breathing it,
you will die.

If you try to understand love
before being held,
you will never feel compassion.

If you insist on bringing God to others
before opening your very small window of life,
you will never have honest friends.

If you try to teach before you learn
or leave before you stay,
you will lose your ability to try.

No matter what anyone promises—
to never feel compassion,
to never have honest friends,
to lose your ability to try—
these are desperate ways to die.

A dog loves the world through its nose.
A fish through its gills.
A bat through its deep sense of blindness.
An eagle through its glide.

And a human life
through its spirit.

ON THE WAY TO CONEY ISLAND

I was eight or nine, rummaging through her basement, through my dead grandfather's books, when she appeared at the foot of the old see-through stairs, nostalgic and moved that I was searching through his things. There were no windows, and the only light came flooding down the length of stairs over her massive shoulders, giving a sheen to her matted gray hair. When I turned, she seemed an immigrant deity. I ran to her with this relic, so worn that the cover was indented with a palm print, the edges crumbling like petrified wood. The book seemed very mysterious. The letters weren't in English but in strange and beautiful configurations. She almost cried and sat on the bottom step. I snuggled between her legs, against her apron. She gathered me in as she opened the relic and said, "This was your grandfather's Talmud. He brought it from Russia." I remember running my little hands all over it the way I do large boulders. Her hands were huge and worked, like moveable stones themselves. She turned me by the shoulders, and with the light flooding my face, she whispered, more firmly than I had ever heard anyone whisper, "You are why we came to this country . . ." She took me by the chin, "You are why I live." She put the relic in my small hands. I was tentative. She gripped me to it firmly, and my small palm slid into the well of my grandfather's touch. She stood on the bottom step, blocking the light, "I love you like life itself." She reached down and sandwiched my little fingers, "These are the oldest things you own." As she waddled up the stairs, the light wavered on and off my face. Without turning, she went back to her kitchen. I stood and the light settled in the impression of Nehemiah's grip, a man I never knew, and I didn't want to leave

26

this dingy threshold. I was afraid to climb back into the light. I stood before those stairs, a grimy little innocent, and felt like an orphan who'd been told I was a prince to a kingdom that had perished before I was born. I leafed through the strange letters, watching the light make glitter of the dust. I put the book behind a secret shelf, afraid it would crumble if brought into the world, and walked the lighted stairs, taller than I had descended. I entered her kitchen older yet still a child and climbed her lap like a throne.

THIS IS IT
(FOR HUGH MACLEAN)

He was a Renaissance scholar,
old-school, rigorous,
and of all the night classes
and office summits,
all I can think of
is that day in spring
when he reduced the Trojan War,
the years of battle and death,
to the stealing of a single apple,
a golden apple that couldn't
be eaten anyway.
And before we could bring
into focus what he was suggesting,
he cupped a brass apple
in his wrinkled hand
and said, "This is it."

We all laughed, but
he didn't move or take
his wizened eyes off the brass apple,
and when our minds went silent,
he said with the soft truth of centuries,
"This is it, Ladies and Gentlemen,
This is it."

I remember the slight dizziness
from just laughing, and how my heart
was pounding, and how I kept flashing—
all our suffering,

from the stealing of an apple
that can't be eaten anyway.
He didn't move, just held
the golden apple before us
with a firm certainty
and no explanation.
It was then that I believed him,
believed him thoroughly.
This was the same apple,
no matter that he brought it
from home, that it weighed him down
all day. I believed him.

That which can't be stolen
but only given,
that which survives
by opening us all,
This is it. Here,
underneath every doubt,
in the center of every question,
at the core of all disciplines,
in the silence that outwaits
all smoke and war.
This is it.

And when the barber told me
that my suited Homer had died
before the azaleas saw the sky,
I realized, this is what he taught me.

All study uncovers it.
All love preserves it.

Nothing else matters.
It is the pit inside every moment.

This is it, Ladies and Gentlemen,
This is it.

THE FEATHER NEVER LANDS

They were the words of a man
who 2600 years ago urged his followers
to rely on their personal experience,
a man whose words have been spun
into 10,000 threads.

I'd waited a long time and searched
for an authentic translation, as if
anything this far down could
resemble his voice. And as I read
in the sun, the soft breeze
unraveled the tensions of my life
and I fell asleep and heard
the lull of an ageless surf,
and he himself came out of the ocean
and we bobbed beyond the breakers,
hardly saying a word, and he merely
ushered me back into my life.

When I woke, I wasn't sure where I was
but the sun through the trees created
patches of light and dark
that were irresistible
and I began to wonder
why birds sing at the first of light,
why crickets cry at a hint of the dark,
why fish nibble at cracks in the deep.

And so it is ours
to sing and cry and nibble our way free.

Don't ask me why—
Just know that humans
sleep before the truth
and learn it nonetheless.

GOD'S WOUNDS

Beyond all that pain has taught
me, the soft well at the base of
time has opened, and life
touching me there
has turned me into a flower
that prays for rain. Now
I understand: to blossom
is to pray, to wilt and shed
is to pray, to turn to mulch
is to pray, to stretch in the dark
is to pray, to break surface
after great months of ice
is to pray, and to squeeze love
up the stalky center toward the
sky with only dreams of color
is to pray, and finally to unfold
again as if never before
is to be the prayer.

One Step Closer

I wonder when my father dies
if all the things he couldn't say will
fly out of him, and mount as a wind
a thousand miles away.

I wonder if his gifts
will leave him, too,
if his ability to build
something out of nothing
will spark another's confidence.

I know I was born to say what he
couldn't, to face what he's turned
from. It's how these things work.
An ecology of Spirit.

For instance, a friend has a toddler
just ten months old, and I can tell
by her deep attention that this
little one has been here before.

I know she will say what I can't find
and face what I can't bear. She
stares at me and I stare back,
our eyes sorting what lives, what
breathes, what gives to air.

How I make hymns of my father's
pain. How my friend's little girl will

make portraits of how I burn.
This is necessary. It's
how Spirit recycles.

We each are born one step closer
to God than those we are born to,
for which we are loved by some
and never forgiven by others.

We each will die with one more
thing to say. We each will wake
with something familiar on our
lip, which we must find
and love.

Carving the Raft into a Flute

Given sincerity, there will be enlightenment.
THE DOCTRINE OF THE MEAN, 200 BC

Of all the things I've seen
after opening my eyes
hundreds of times a day
for hundreds of days,
any one will do,
for it is in the empty glass
as well as the full, and early light
which is only early to us, warms
the mouth of a simpleton
as well as a scientist,
and the wind up from nowhere
stirs the dead tree as cleanly
as the living.

Of all the things I've thought
while undressing when tired,
the ones that tell me I am alive
have been there all along.
Only something particular
like my lover's far off look at dawn
reminds me that today
is yet to happen.

Of all the times
I thought I liked this
or didn't care for that,

not one was of my choosing
or yours, for as the Earth
was begun like a dish breaking,
Eternity is that scene slowly
reversing, and you and I
and the things we are drawn to
are merely the pieces of God
unbreaking back together.

EARTH PRAYER

O Endless Creator, Force of Life, Seat of the Unconscious,
Dharma, Atman, Ra, Qalb, Dear Center of our Love,
Christlight, Yaweh, Allah, Mawu,
Mother of the Universe . . .

Let us, when swimming with the stream,
become the stream.
Let us, when moving with the music,
become the music.
Let us, when rocking the wounded,
become the suffering.

Let us live deep enough
till there is only one direction,
and slow enough till there is only
the beginning of time,
and loud enough in our hearts
till there is no need to speak.

Let us live for the grace beneath all we want,
let us see it in everything and everyone,
till we admit to the mystery
that when I look deep enough into you,
I find me, and when you dare to hear my fear
in the recess of your heart, you recognize it
as your secret which you thought
no one else knew.

O let us embrace
that unexpected moment of unity

as the atom of God.
Let us have the courage
to hold each other when we break
and worship what unfolds . . .

O nameless spirit that is not done with us,
let us love without a net
beyond the fear of death
until the speck of peace
we guard so well
becomes the world.

Things No One Asks About

I have been called heroic
for merely surviving,
which is like championing an eagle
for flying to its nest

and I have been condemned as selfish
for following the call of truth,
which is like blaming a turtle
for finding the deep

and I have escaped death more than once
but not the dying.

§

I have been worn slowly by experience
and torn apart instantly by crisis and revelation
and all I can say is Life is Food:
to love is to chew; to forgive,
to swallow.

I cough up these bits:
the heart like a wing
is of no use tucked
and distrust in the world
like an eye swollen shut
stops the work of love.

§

Like a worried glassblower
trying to refigure his clear and shattered heart,
I have cut myself on all that I was,
surprised at the wisdom
hiding in the edges.

AT THE WINDOW

I was at the window
when a fly near the latch
was on its back spinning—
legs furious, going nowhere.

I thought to swat it
but something in its struggle
was too much my own.

It kept spinning and began to tire.
Without moving closer, I exhaled
steadily, my breath a sudden wind,
and the fly found its legs,
rubbed its face
and flew away.

I continued to stare at the latch
hoping that someday, the breath
of something incomprehensible
would right me and
enable me to fly.

LET'S VOICE THE POSSIBILITIES

In a world filled with mystery and ruin,
you can leave the house certain of who
you are and return fatigued, only to
have some ancient spirit whisper
in your ear, "If you let me near,
you will taste the sweetest part
of being here."

And the next day, you can remember
something essential while fiddling
with the radio at a stop light.

So, let's voice the possibilities.
If you fly, you will be seen,
for your wings are powerful
and full of color. If not, you
will miss why you are here.

What does it mean to fly? Well,
that's the question, isn't it?

For those of us wanting to be loved,
it's the courage to say,
I am lonely.

For those of us tumbling in our
fear, it's the courage to accept
that nothing is certain
but still to know—

in this open wing
that is our breath—
we are safe.

Fire in the Temple

In everything, I seek to grasp the fundamental.
BORIS PASTERNAK

I believe what the self centered have torn down,
the other-centered will build up.
MARTIN LUTHER KING, JR.

THE SECRET IS BURNING

but I can't tell if it's using us up or lighting
the way. Back from Prague, I tell my father
of the Jewish Cemetery so strangely full of
life and ask if he had to hide being a Jew.
He says, "Of course. A nail sticking up
will get hammered." At 89, he can barely
walk, has set up chairs in all the rooms, so
he can look for where he left the secret. He
says, "The places get shorter. The time takes
longer. You do the best with what you've got."
Now he talks of his mother's mother coming to
live with them after Treblinka. Her brother ran
to Israel to put out the secret, only to become a
thief. My father says, "The war let a darkness out
of him he couldn't get back in." Now he's talking
about the cot he slept on as a boy, set up in the
bathtub in case the secret started to burn while
he slept. After the Pogroms, his grandfather
landed on Canal Street where he made boxes
for jewelry, neatly covered with leather, and his
mother as a young woman sewed velvet inside
so soft you could keep the secret there for a
thousand years. He doesn't know that I'm
holding the mezuzah she carried across the
ocean. His voice begins to tire and the secret
starts to smoke under his tongue. Oh father,
I've spent my life making small containers to
carry what matters. But I've let the secret
stay a secret. It's what the secret wants.

For us to taste it, not to spill it. It's
made me love the bent nail you are.

THE FINITUDES

It's taken almost sixty years, but I've
stopped figuring out what people want. Now
I try to let light pass between us, which when
it happens feels like love. Today I stumble on
Heidegger's notion of dwelling with care in the
being that underlies everything. Feel myself say-
ing yes. Only to discover he supported Hitler and
enforced Aryan law as rector of the University
of Freiburg. Effusive telegrams to Hitler, and
turning in Jewish professors. Now being shaped
by what people want seems trivial. Or is resisting
this the DNA of conscience? Hannah Arendt, his
student and lover, was a Jew. She testified on his
behalf. How are we to hold such contradictions?
Somewhere seeds are being watered until they
break ground and somewhere flesh is burning.
This is hard enough to take in. How does this
happen in the same person without their soul
exploding? We've all been taught to take what
we need and leave the rest. Why not drink from
Heidegger's being and push the rest away? But
the pushed-away parts evolve too. I'm trying to
absorb what we've done to each other, trying
to eat all of what I see and scrub one
thing back to the beginning.

FIRE IN THE TEMPLE

*Sokuhi (1616–1671) was a Buddhist monk and an
accomplished poet and calligrapher. Along with Mokuan (1611–
1684) and their teacher, Yuan (1592–1673), the three were
known in Japan as the "Three Brushes of Ōbaku" (Ōbaku
no Sanpitsu). In 1650 at the age of thirty-four, Sokuhi was
badly burned while fighting a forest fire near the temple and
nearly died from asphyxiation. In the midst of the fire, he was
suddenly enlightened. He lived for twenty-one more years.*

There I was, unsure if the fire was supposed to
fill the temple the way life fills a body. Others were
frantic, swatting robes at the base of flames, but I
was stopped by the beauty of the yellow heat em-
bracing the trees. It made me think of my father's
funeral pyre. Where did the fire take him? In the
heart's long look back, I wanted to run into the
flames and go after him. There's something in us
that wants to join the flame. It was then master
Yuan stood before me, flames everywhere, the
forest crackling, the empty temple waiting, master
Yuan calm as the lake before dawn. He spoke softly,
"Now you have to choose, Sokuhi." A burning limb
fell behind us. He stepped closer, "Will you bring
in there out here? Or keep watching from the rim?"
His robe caught aflame and I cried out, knock-
ing him to the ground, smothering the heat.
Though his back was burned, he stared into
the small fire I'd been guarding inside for
years. Something in the truth of his love

brought me into the world. I began to weep.
The flames moved past us closer to the temple.
I ran through them to get more water and the
smoke of centuries made my eyes burn and the
veil between worlds made my legs heavy. I couldn't
breathe. I grew light-headed in the midst of flames
taller than the temple and began to sing some
song that rose from my small fire so eager to
join the fire around us. I didn't understand
what was happening. But the harder it was to
breathe, the more I understood my breath. The
harder it was to keep my eyes open, the more I
understood the moment of true seeing. The last
thing I saw was the temple waiting for the flames.
When I came to, the earth had been cleared and
the temple seemed less a refuge and more an oasis.

THINGS CARRIED
THROUGH THE FIRE

My grandfather's Talmud.
Your picture of Uncle Billy.
The innocence of our dog.
The things I never show the
world. The things I never show
myself. The things we believe in.
The dream I no longer need.
The uncertainty at the center
of all my plans. The small flame
that keeps changing names. Now
the days burn like bones, slowly
and all at once. And what we
thought would last burns like
wax. Under it, everything.

ROAD TRIP

A bird hits a window in a tower
in Dallas, startling a man at his
desk. A bit of feather and blood
is stuck there. He calls maintenance
but no one comes. It's all he can see.
He doesn't want to die while filling
out another form. In the same mo-
ment, an old rancher in Montana
drops his hammer while nailing a
fence his father built. As he dies,
the extra nails fall from his mouth.
In the same moment, a waitress in
New Hampshire, late for work, thinks
she might rush that left turn off Route
13, but she waits. While waiting, a fox
appears in the snow. She's never seen
a fox. As she makes the turn, the fox
disappears and the canopy of maples,
growing toward each other for years,
welcomes her to a timeless place
where windows and fences and
rushing can't go.

If You Want a True Friend

Just open your hands and say, "I don't know."
Say it softly and wait, so your other can see
that you mean it. Give them a chance to
drop what they think is secret. Let them
come up with a cup of what matters from
the spring they show no one. Let them sigh
and admit that they don't know either. Then
you can begin with nothing in the way. Go
on. Admit to the throb you carry in your
heart. And let the journey begin.

THE GREAT OPENING

Act always as if the future of the Universe depends
on what you do, while laughing at yourself for thinking
that whatever you do makes any difference.

BUDDHA

I want to learn more and more to see as beautiful what is necessary . . .
then I shall be one of those who makes things beautiful.

NIETZSCHE

CAUGHT IN THE RAIN

I saw a woman sitting in a café
in Barcelona. She had the loneliest
stare. She fiddled with her espresso
for the longest time. Then I took
in everyone and realized we're all
still-lifes waiting to be finished
by our next meeting.

It takes a quiet courage to slip
from our regrets the way you
might step from wet clothes
after being caught in the rain.

What is it about these flowers
trampled by a horse? Or the broken
glass being swept by the old woman?
Or the time I chanced to see a hawk
break through a cloud? Everything
I see, I've been or will be.

Don't Give Up on Me

I am so myself now that when I open,
I become what I meet, for a while, and
then, as a drop of wine recolors a glass
of water, I am redone and made anew.
Then I wait for someone to drink of me.
And so it goes. We're all taste and swallow.
Out to quench what can't be quenched.
Still something swirls deep within me like
the slow death of my father who calls every
month to share the ping of all he's hidden.
Our love drops like a pebble now into the
long well our suffering has made. And
when I least expect it, I'm not myself or
anyone I know. I start to drown in every-
thing magnificent. Being alive can get this
choppy. But I have friends I climb like a
raft. I want to be such a raft. Even more,
a clear lake in which those who swim
can know themselves better.

TAKING TURNS

Our sweet dog Mira has an eye infection and so each day for a week, three times a day, we take turns, calling her to the kitchen where she sits against the cabinet as we hold a warm compress to her sore eye. Today, it's my turn. The sun is rising and I'm on my knees, holding her head, as she looks up at me with her other eye. This is what ailments do: they bring us to our knees where we can hold each other's head and finally, in the quiet before the day begins, we can look into each other's one good eye. Now compassion rises like a very light bird fluttering in my throat. I think it wants to fly into the world. I want it to, but it hovers there, keeping everything connected, as if fluttering in our throat is its home.

EVIDENT

Why do I keep putting everything away?
I need to be distracted by what matters,
to leave the Seferis poems open to the one
about the old man and the river, to put my
unfinished woodblock of the heron lifting
before the waterfall on my desk, shavings
and all, where I can chisel a stroke as I
pass by, to set the journal I travel with
by my bed, open to the secret I haven't
figured out that I heard in the halyard
slapping the mast in Sausalito. I need
to start more things than I can finish,
to leave the twine of my feelings around
the house where you can find them and
ask, "What is this?" How can I fear there
is not enough time when the openings
that have changed my life have
only taken a moment?

WHERE WE
NEED TO BE

It isn't long after we arrive
that everyone starts pointing
and telling us where we need
to be and what we need to do
to get there. There's no time
to really ask why. Soon, things
happen and we're thrown off
course and now there's all this
effort to win their approval. If
lucky, love will distract us more
than suffering. If blessed, we're
broken of everyone's plans and
regrets and thrown like a hooded
bird into a sea of light. If trust-
ing the fall, we find our wings.

KNOWING, DRINKING, AND SEEKING

Without knowing who I am—
that is, without finding the place
where God and I join—I will
become everyone I love.

Without drinking from the quiet—
that is, without listening for the place
from which all living things speak—
I will talk too much and wonder
why I'm not heard.

Without seeking the self that lives
beneath all names, all my attempts
at kindness will fail, for everything
I do will turn everyone in need
into me.

This being human is a series of
blindnesses that come and go.
But we can outlive our mistakes,
for the mysterious river is always
near and greater than our thirst.

THE AFTERMATH OF RAIN

Something beneath all doubt tells me that I must look or I will die. This need to look makes me lean into everything with passion. It makes me speak to you. It makes me stand before small gatherings and utter my deepest questions before strangers who once hearing are no longer strangers. When we enter our questions, the voicings heard pluck the voicings unheard, and a delicate music begins that is both open and secret at once. In the silence that follows, it's unclear who is speaking and who is listening. I must look or I will die. It is somehow written in my heart. I must say what I see or I will not be fully alive. No one taught me this. Each of us, in our own way, is born to draw the unseeable out of the ordinary, striking our inwardness like a drum that somehow keeps the soul of the world going. Like it or not, we are seers and sayers who keep drumming what is in, out. All of us blessed and cursed to keep the feet of God dancing.

GEMSEED

Loving yourself is like
feeding a clear bird
no one else can see.

You must be still and offer
your palmful of secrets
like delicate seed.

As she eats your secrets
no longer secret
she glows
and you lighten
and her voice
which only you can hear
is your voice
bereft of plans.

And the light
through her body
will bathe you
till you wonder
why the gems in your palm
were ever fisted.

Others will think you crazed
to wait on something
no one sees.

But the clear bird
only wants to feed
and fly and sing.

She only wants
light in her belly.

And once in a great while
if someone loves you enough
they might see her rise
from the nest
beneath your fear.

THE ONE THING

There's this one thing
I can't remember or can't
quite find. On gray days,
I worry I've misplaced it or
my memory is failing. But
on days like today when
everything is swelling with
life, I'm certain it's always
been this way. To sense such
a thing without finding it is
what keeps us reaching for
each other. I'm coming to
believe it's not about finding
anything. More about the
treasures we discover by
opening what seems
in the way. Whatever
we find is what we've
been looking for.

WHAT HOLDS US

At first we might feel the self
like a rock packed in the earth
after a long rain. Then we might
settle into the pouch of the Uni-
verse like a starfish tucked in the
sand of a night sea. This might
give way till we flutter like a baby
bird in the hand of God. In the
deepest sitting, God might feel
like a baby bird fluttering in your
hand. And then there may be no
you, no hand, no God. Then all
of God may be in you.

RELEASING BEAUTY

Spirit waits in everything like the
incandescent shimmer between electrons.
Each time we're drawn to create, it's the
shimmer that recreates us. Each time we
shape something out of nothing, the heart
stirs like a red bird remembering it was
meant to fly. Each time we give when no
one is looking, we peel what covers our
timeless center. When softened this
way, silence reaches through us till we
admit we are chimes carrying an ancient
song. "Then why try so hard?" you ask.
Because trying is singing, too. Because
sweat exercises the dream. After so much
work, we think we've produced something
that never existed, when it is we who wake
closer to what never dies. Whatever stirs
us to put together the few things we find,
it is we who flower from giving away
the nectar of our being.

She's Next to Me Now

Our Mira is ten. Her face beginning
to whiten. She sleeps on us whenever
she can. I love to watch her golden
lashes flutter as she dreams. I can't
bear to think of her dying. Can't
imagine her not at the door bring-
ing a toy and shimmying between
my legs. We went today for a long
walk in the pines, in the snow, and
time seemed to part like a great white
wave. We saw no one. Just she with
snow on her nose, running ahead and
looking back, wondering what's
taking us so long.

TO GLOW

Like light in the sun
spilling out of the sun,
the spirit within
beams its way
through all our cracks
till our most treasured
walls come down.

The coming down
of those walls is the
blessing we crave
and resist.

The coming down of
those walls—so the light
of the soul like the light
of the sun can help the
world grow—this is
the call of calls.

An Open Hand

The mind is not a storeroom
with mirrors where we retreat
to convince ourselves
that we exist.

The mind is a livingroom with
windows and more than one chair,
so friends can come and look out
and discuss what they see.

Not a fortress where we frisk and
strip others of what they believe
in order to share our secrets.

More a porch with birdfeeders
and coffee or tea where before
hello, you have to share a story.

Pull the curtains! Open the
windows! Brew the coffee!
Put out a sign: Other Views
Wanted!

LEAST COMPLICATED

Sometimes I go about pitying myself,
and all the time I am being carried
on great winds across the sky.
OJIBWAY SAYING

Sometimes I lose it, like the keys to
the car left in my jeans after that long
walk through the pines when I fell into
the marsh and the keys were all muddy,
caked in my pocket, then tossed in the
washing machine. Then you called and
there was dinner and the bills. And I
couldn't find them and felt that rush
of loss as if I'd left my heart out in the
rain and it washed away. How will I get
anywhere? Where will I look for my heart?
The truth never really goes away, just deeper
within like a turtle pulling back into its shell.
When afraid, I carry my better self like a glass
of water balanced on a tray and startled, I spill
it and try to gather it on the floor. But once
I've made my mess and tossed the keys and
lost my heart and spilled my better self on
everything, somehow I am brought back.
Then I ache to simply feel what I can't under-
stand. Then I stand in the rain and brush
the mud from my eyes and laugh. The keys
have been in my pocket the whole time.

SAMPLE BOARDS

You taught me to keep a chisel sharp.
You showed me on old pine, always the
sample board. "Don't stop in mid-stroke
or the board will splinter." "Once you start,
keep pushing through." You'd pick up the
perfect shaving from the floor and rub it
between your fingers. Your other hand
would rub the grain revealed. How you'd
smile. You went somewhere unreachable.
When I read Plato years later, all his squawk
about absolute forms, I knew that's where you
went. You'd rub the clean cut and drop the
shaving. I loved to watch the feather of wood
float to the basement floor. Of course, keeping
things sharp and cut hasn't always worked out.
You were 89 when you sent me your chisels.
You couldn't steady them anymore. You
sharpened them before taping the box.
And I no longer know what it is we
build: the cut, each other, the grain
inside, or is it all for the light-
ness that floats between us?

GOING INWARD

I've been walking the acre
of my soul. It's been so long.
And over there, the hill I used to
sit on. I'd watch the stars reflect
in the river when it was tired of
running. I wonder what the view
is now. But it takes at least a day
to get there and another to sit still
in the grass and another to wait for
the stars to come out and another
for the river to tire. Sure, life keeps
taking us away. But the only time
I'm free of fear is when I drink
from that river.

GOING HOME

It was the middle of the day.
Early September. Light skirting
from under the leaves. I was taking
the compost to the edge of the yard
when I saw you pinching a pot on
the old bench near the birdbath
we'd lugged from Albany. Mira was
lying in the grass, sun closing her
eyes. Something in the quiet light
made me realize that we were now,
in this moment, all we'd hoped for.
I put the can down and sat next to
you. Watched your hands shape
the clay. I wanted to run my fingers
through your hair. A small cloud
bowed and the sun warmed my
hand on your knee.

RELIC FROM THE FUTURE

Questions found on an antique cell phone
discovered in 2086 in the ruins of an airport
when people traveled by plane: What if I let
love in all the way? Why am I always leaving?
What is it that stirs me about being caught?
Though I never wanted safe, why have I settled
for safe? Why do I keep running, when I have
no interest in moving? How do I say yes more
often? How do I stop reliving the past? How can
I learn to use my freedom? Having lived most of
my life in fear of what's coming, how can I find
meaning where I am? How can I stop playing
small? How can I put down the upset of not
getting what I want? How can I better see the
unseen? How can I die to old ways of being?
How can I let what wants to be born in me
have its way? Now that I've been helped,
how can I find the strength to help others?
Just what is my work? And what will it
take to taste the honey?

FOR YOUR BIRTHDAY

You ask for a story instead of a present and
I've fallen into remembering the moment I
knew I couldn't live without you. We'd just
finished lunch, early on. It was fall. We were
saying goodbye on the corner of Madison and
Robin. The wind lifted your hair as you smiled.
I've always loved your smile. As you turned and
crossed the street, I felt something tug and ache.
I wanted to reach for you, to say with urgency—
Don't go. Don't ever go. But it was only after
lunch, early on. So I watched you go. I've come
to understand that in that simple moment, I felt
the whole of our life together. On that corner,
it felt like a thumb pressing on the center of my
heart. It stopped my breathing for a second and
in that pause, I knew I had to see you again.
Through the years, I've felt my heart indent
that way a handful of times: carrying popcorn
into a theatre and hearing you laugh, seeing
you work wet clay in the yard as yellow leaves
fall, watching you watch the moon above the
winter trees, coming home to see you drip
water from your finger into the mouth a
broken bird. What kind of story is this?
I know you better than anyone and yet
something in you makes me want to
hold you and ask, who are you now?

UPSTREAM

When it is we who do
the stepping, it's hard
to see the steps. But
look where you are.

Years ago, the gift
you carried since birth
was waiting inside
for you.

This very day you're
bringing what you
carried through the
fire into the world.

Even more, you've
become the cup that
holds your soul.

You fit your gift.
Your gift fits you. It
doesn't matter if you have
everything in place. Slow
and live this day. You
have earned this view.

BEFORE THE TWICE-LOCKED GATES

I speak to you from a land where elders have shown their grandchildren how to sing their way through. I speak this in a land where skin pounds skin. From the outside in, we call this brutality. From the inside out, we call this song. The gift of Africa tells us that song is the only thing that can outlast brutality. Whether you suffer an unjust system or an oppressive father, whether you have been in a prison of another's making or in a cage of your own construction, this sun-baked continent that carries the tremor of the beginning tells any who will listen that song is the only thing that can outlast brutality. The drums, if leaned into, will carry you along. The drums, which have no beginning or end, will circle you through the many faces of pain and joy. The drums sound the heartbeat of God, clear and unending. Even when oppressed to the point of silence, the drumbeat cannot be silenced. Even if you are born a *funé,* a storyteller who is not permitted to sing, there is song in how you raise your eyes to the unwatched sky. Even if you are forbidden to cry your truth, there is the *Geuca Solo,* the dance without words before the twice-locked gates. Pain held in is pain. Pain let out is dance. Worry held in is worry. Worry let out is the cry of a bird that lives on the branch of heart that no one sees. Sorrow held in is sorrow. But sorrow let out is the song of the continents moving together. Even if you are forbidden to cry your truth, there is still the dance without words before the twice-locked gates. No matter if the gates are generations old, no matter if the gates are in your mind, no matter if when you move, you stumble. It is the gift of Africa for the children of the Earth: God is the wood in the drums, drums sound the heartbeat of the living, song is the thing that will outlast brutality . . .

TIDAL

I have held the dying,
have felt their life surge one last time
like a surf, have held those not even
a day old, have seen their eyes flicker
out of focus at the coolness
of this thing called air,
and I have been the dying,
held until I came back.

I have been crushed to center
and left for invisible, and played
like a sweet thing with broken strings,
and in the hush after truth is shared,
in the wake of all explanation and excuse,
in the aftermath of illusions snapped
like sticks, nothing matters now
but the instant where all I am
mounts like a wave for you,
the instant my hand parts
the air between us.

I tell you I have come so close
to death that I forgot my name
and now all names seem useless.

So nothing matters but emptying
till the softness we call Spirit bubbles
through the tongue and words fail
in utter adoration. Nothing now

but this need to be . . . naked
in the midst of what we feel.

THE GREAT OPENING

It was the son of a soldier,
a soldier who killed his own people.
It was that gentle son who went
in despair to his grandfather's
bridge to ask in his
solitude why.

And that night he dreamt
that everyone who'd been hurt
and everyone who'd done the hurting
met on that bridge. And in their
awkwardness and pain, it began
to rain flowers which grazing
their skin opened their faces
and they were healed.

And the flowers, falling
into the water, brought
the fish who thought
the petals were food.

And the son of the soldier
woke committed to the building
of bridges and to the food
of flowers raining
from the sky.

BEING A FEATHER

He sat quietly
as his father went silent.
Sometimes, his father
would look far off and
the shape of his eyes
would sag, and he knew
his father was carrying
the things that burn
where no one can speak.

It was then that the feather
appeared. He tried to guess
if it was hawk or crow or
maybe heron, but his father
said, "It doesn't matter
from which flying thing
it comes. What matters
is that it carries us back
and forth into the life above
and the life below."

His father held the feather
as if it were his own,
"It carries us into sky life,
then ground life until
both are home."

His father placed the feather
in his hands, "Anything

that connects above and
below is such a feather.
The quiet is such a feather.
Pain is such a feather.
Friendship is such a feather.
The things that burn
where no one can speak
is such a feather. You
are such a feather."

BEYOND MEASURE

Having burned dreams to keep warm,
I think of dreams as kindling now.
Having carried loved ones as far as I
could to the other side, I make your
coffee and bring you a tissue, as if
these gestures open us to Heaven.

Because they do.

Having outlasted the noise in my
head and yours, I can at times hear
the breath of life between our
disappointments.

Meeting this way, more than halfway
through, I ask different questions. Not,
"Where are you going?" But, "How did
you come to here?" And, "Have you
opened the treasure before you?"
"And, if so, can you teach me?"

UTTERANCE-THAT-RISES-BRIEFLY-FROM-THE-SOURCE

Peace is an odd word for the bubble of all there is
breaking repeatedly on the surface of the heart,
but I know of no other. The Native Americans
come closest; nothing between inner events
and what to call them. I see you and you always
glow. Why not call you One-who-shines-like-a-
sun-upon-first-meeting. Why not call the moment
of doubt and fear: Dark-point-spinning-loose-
that-presses-on-the-throat. Why not call the
moment of certainty, the fleeting moment
when everything that ever lived is right
behind my pounding heart, why not call
that moment: Beat-of-the-thousand-wings-
of-God-inside-my-chest. When I feel love so
deeply that I can't bear it, when I feel it so much
that it can't be contained or directed at any one
thing or person, why not call it: The-stone-at-the-
bottom-of-the-river-sings. Why not call you: The-
hand-that-plucks-me-from-the-bottom-of-the-river.
Why not call this miracle of life: The-sound-that-
never-stops-stirring-the-lost-within-the-sound-that-
never-stops-soothing-the-living-within-the-sound-that-
never-stops-sounding-in-the-eyes-of-dead-things-coming-
alive-again-and-again-and-again . . .

Suite for the Living

When you find your place where you are,
practice occurs.

DOGEN

Suite for the Living

1. Endgame

Death pushed me to the edge.
Nowhere to back off. And
to the shame of my fears,
I danced with abandon
in his face. I never
danced as free.

And Death backed off,
the way dark backs off
a sudden burst of flame.
Now there's nothing left
but to keep dancing.

It is the way
I would have chosen
had I been born
three times
as brave.

2. Tell Me
You Have Come

There is a timing
larger than any of us, a
readiness that comes and goes
like the heat that makes
our secret walls melt.

How many times have I passed
exactly what I need, only
noticing the stream
when troubled by thirst.

The mystery is that
whoever shows up
when we dare to give
has exactly what we need
hidden in their trouble.

3. Advice That's Hard to Take

When you pace at the edge of life,
worried and afraid, mount your will
like an arrow of salt
and plunge into
the ocean of experience.

4. ACEQUIA

Only when the fish let go
their dream of having arms
did they grow their magnificent fins.

5. Practicing

As a man in his last breath
drops all he is carrying

each breath is a little death
that can set us free.

6. FREEFALL

If you have one hour of air
and many hours to go,
you must breathe slowly.

If you have one arm's length
and many things to care for,
you must give freely.

If you have one chance to know God
and many doubts, you must
set your heart on fire.

We are blessed.

Each day is a chance.
We have two arms.
Fear wastes air.

BOOK TWO

INHABITING WONDER

for those
who search their hearts
while listening
to the wind

TIME IS A GARDEN

Things that matter take time to root and meaning takes time to blossom. Though we forget, time is a garden in which each of us is a seed breaking surface when we're born. In wonder, we start to tend and water the things we dream of and care about. But as the seasons pass, we discover that we are the ones being watered and grown. Early on, we're in a hurry, not wanting to miss anything, eager for the horizon. Then we trip and fall and are forced to touch the earth again. Soon, we're wanting time to slow, wanting every moment to last, wanting to watch the orchid every day as it inches open, knowing our soul is opening in just this way.

Like it or not, a deep part of our journey is to stay engaged in life long enough for truth to show itself. In spite of how we race to tomorrow, time speaks by how things grow, change, and evolve around us. Eventually, the fallen tree across a stream diverts the water to irrigate the field, fulfilling its purpose. The wooden stairs in an old farm house are worn by the generations of feet that walk them. If we stand in their steps and listen, we can hear their stories. And the faces of the medieval angels painted on the church walls in Italy are worn of their features over centuries, confirming that we're all at heart the same, if we can stop and go beneath our personal history.

In essence, poetry offers us a way to listen to time. When we can stop and open our heart, poetry lets us enter time and not just move through it. When we can enter time, we find that Eternity is the experience of all life in any given moment and not the endless stacking of years. Mysteriously, when we can stop and open, the past, present, and future are always before us, speaking as one unnameable energy. So when we see an old woman on the street, it's entering time that lets us see her as a young woman too.

The sections in the second book in this collection explore how kindness, truth, and softness help us to enter time and inhabit wonder. In the section "The Keepers of Kindness," the poems bear witness to the ways we give because it's in our nature, and how kindness always restores our kinship with life. In the section "Letting What Is Shine," the poems affirm the hard practice of seeing things as they are, and how the bare is-ness of life is the source of resilience. In the section "In," the poems look closely at the nature of inner life and inner knowing. And in the section "Softer than Truth," the poems bow to the gifts of tenderness and vulnerability that let us join with life and not just watch it.

THE KEEPERS OF KINDNESS

In the 1600s, the Japanese master Basho spoke to his student, Kikakou:

We shouldn't abuse God's creatures.
You must reverse your haiku.

Not:

a dragonfly;
remove its wings—
pepper tree.

But:

pepper tree;
add wings to it—
dragonfly.

The world depends on which way
this thought unfolds.

INSIDE THE DRUM

Time is the great sifter
we all resist.

And I confess, I have loved
the things that can't love back
until my appetite for confusion
has sifted away.

Now, for all the search,
I have landed where I am
and the thousand answers I
have carried have broken open
to the few questions
that sustain.

How is it possible:
the mud of agitation has sifted.
Now I drift in the slow, clear water
with nothing to do but wake,
drink, love, and give away.

BENEATH ALL TROUBLE, ONENESS

When I saw the wheelchair man
with spindly limbs twist his neck to the sun,
I wanted to take the newborn from the blanket
and put her in his hands.

And when the blind woman knelt at the stoplight
to hug her dog, I wanted to embrace everyone
who ever showed me an inch of truth.

There is less and less between heart and world.
In the morning, I am sure
this is a deep blessing.
By night, it seems a curse.

In time, our pains in being here
crack open into a soft wonder
that no one owns.

I notice everything now, and more,
I am everything I notice.

Like one who suddenly sees while staring,
I now know love, though I have been loving.

To watch the sun rim your face,
your head in my lap, while small birds sing—
I could have died there on that bench,
but want so much to live.

Can it be—
as blood needs veins to do its work,
love needs us?

ACROSS THE STREET

I'm walking in Manhattan when across the street a blind woman catches the tip of her cane in a break in the sidewalk and falls, quickly, with no chance to brace herself. It's a hard fall. She scrapes her face and legs. And in the moment of her fall, she lets out a cry so honest and painful, so full of the realization that she is falling with no way to brace herself, a cry so full of forced surrender that everyone within a hundred feet freezes—stops what they're doing, stops thinking of where they're going. We're pulled from the busyness of our private isolations. Her cry cuts through our layers of difference, through all the ways we dream and survive. All doing stops, all reasoning stops, all walls are run through. Her blind, unguarded utterance touches the common cry sleeping in each of us.

As she falls, we are her, and the webs of philosophy and culture are ripped like a screen torn by a storm. For a moment, the unseeable lightning of what it means to be human strikes through her, charging its way through the rest of us. I watch, my heart pounding in my throat, as someone helps her up. All the codes to live by come down to this—helping each other up. We all watch. No one can move. And I want to look every stranger—stopped like me—in the eye. Without ever knowing their names, I want to feel this admission of Oneness against our wills.

But soon, we begin to shuffle and assume our learned differences, readjusting to our busyness, and life in its paradoxical smallness begins again. The buzz of the street resumes. I cross traffic slowly and stand in front of the blind woman just set back into the stream. Speechless, I want to offer something and touch her arm. She pulls away and taps her cane on the concrete as my heart pounds in my ears.

SELF-EMPLOYMENT

Everyone we meet is a friend
carrying a gift. Our job, to listen
the friend open, the way the sun
listens a stalk into a peony.

Every day has a gift, a piece of food
to keep you going, a truth hidden in
a corner to remind you of your life
about to be lived, a cloth someone
discarded that will keep you warm.
Our job, to love the piece
of gift we find.

The hardest thing is to keep
looking when your heart is broken,
to keep listening when your body is
hurting and violence is all around.
But this is when the gifts are closest,
in the warmth of soup that finds
you coming out of the cold.

WHAT HAPPENS OTHERWISE

Now that I'm the tortoise, I can see—
sometimes my need to know
is greater than my ability to wait
and so I arrive at notions prematurely,
like spilled paints cleaned up
before they have time
to find their shapes.

Like the spread of silence
stopped by words, I
cut the journey short.

What happens otherwise
when I am still or confused
is that a moment—like being
wheeled into surgery—changes
everything, and ten years later,
another—like standing under
the African moon—rearranges
my voice, and three years after,
waiting in the rain for a light
to turn, I cry for the first
and understand the second.

When we can keep
from interfering,
the fired bits
become who we are
and the necklace forms.

THOUGH LOSS
IS EVERYWHERE

Your mother has died and you feel her
tenderness everywhere you turn. You reach
for her and come up empty. You long to pick
up the phone and call. You look for things
of hers to hold. But the dearest thing she
held was you. Perhaps her greatest gift
in going is that to feel her now,
you have to hold yourself.

You ask how I can go on? Why don't
I have regrets? I guess I've been worn
to where I no longer reach. This is
neither better or worse. This is just
how it's happened to me. I am not
removed. I just feel like a pebble
scoured in the bottom of the stream.

The losses hurt and I struggle too,
to stay in the light, to get up and
try again. But the shore crumbling
into its beauty gives me strength.

Like the sun which changes everything,
those we love vanish, but their light
returns as another day,
like it or not.

So open your hand that has held
so much. What it has known
now lives in you, in a place
you can't always reach.

I will hold you every chance I get
but this won't compare to holding
yourself. Perhaps grief is how we exhaust
our reach for things that have gone,
and acceptance is how we slowly
learn to hold ourselves in
the middle of the storm.

SURF

I settle into the heat of a dune
to watch an old surfer. He paddles
and waits to catch the next wave,
which he rides with great balance
till the wave slips back under like an
invisible whale. I watch him do this
several times and realize that catch-
ing the next wave is key, and slipping
off the thing that carries you just
before it throws you under is just
as key. I lean my head back in the
sand and know the wave I've been
riding is coming to an end. It's been
a good ride. But soon I'll have to slip
off, not to be thrown under. How will
I know? The surfer is gone. The waves
rise for long stretches before slipping
out of view. I find myself talking
to the sea.

Sometimes a Great Cleansing

We are such strangers to the Mystery
that we mistake any depth of feeling
for sadness, any sense of the unknown
for fear, and any sense of peace for boredom.

So when the piano reaches me,
I close my eyes and try to keep the chord
on my tongue till it enters my blood, till
whatever words I finally utter look
like stars to the dark place
that sent me searching.

Such immersion awakens freedom, not
freedom of choice or freedom to vote, but
freedom to float without guilt on the
human sea, freedom to rest like
an old stone full of heat.

Sometimes it takes a great raucous
cleansing to open the chambers
of the soul. And often, we mistake
such cleansing as crisis or betrayal.

But God scours our infidelities
of conscience the way floods rush
ditches, and we are forced to tremble
in aftermath, barely born.

How Not to Abdicate

When decisions complicate,
try to go below them
where the job is simply
to go on breathing.

If in pain, the task
is to remove
what is paining you.

If you can't, the work
must go the other way,
till you soften and enlarge
like water around
whatever strikes it.

When events seem too
important, resist the
pull to yes or no.

If someone presses
left or right, take
an unmarked way.

When the egoists whittle
at everything larger than
themselves, be with things
that can't talk.

When nothing seems to
matter, find early light
and stand like a tree
in the wind.

Stay this way
long after your arms tire.
Stay this way
until you are unsure
what "matter" even means.

Pretend you have roots
and be still, despite the urge
to run, and things that are
alive will find you.

ABOVE AND BELOW

Before I could speak, I reached
for something shiny. And godlike
figures swooping in from nowhere
blew small winds in my ear.

Later my parents tried to tell me
there was no wind. It was our relatives
playing with me in my crib. But I know
better. For over the years I've been re-
arranged by movements of air. And kept
alive more than once by godlike things
swooping in from nowhere.

You see, things are always what they
seem and more. Like icebergs, above
and below. Like what we say. And what
happens to us. Like the ribbon of to-
morrow behind the winter trees this
instant. Just another day *and* the call
of all that is waiting out of view.

So when I chance upon an infant,
I lean in close and close my eyes, let-
ting all the love I've known and dreamt
rise from the basin of my being. Until it
rounds the soft precipice of my mouth
and falls as a whisper that might
steer a life toward light when lost.

UNLESS

Unless exhausted of my plans,
I won't hear the wisdom in your pain.
Unless you stop rehearsing your worry,
you won't feel how life is lifting us. When
unencumbered, we can sense where we
belong. Under all our trouble, we're
connected like the children of
immigrants dreaming of each
other a continent away.

CROSSINGS

Everywhere, what is inner
is bursting to become outer:
the yellow of daffodils inches up
their stems, while the wings of
unborn eagles stir inside their
eggs, and the feelings of children
begin to sprout language, as the
water in the ocean swells and
spits and sprays and tries to
leave itself—this is the source
of waves, the source of their
beauty—that they can't.

It's how we love.

JOINING THE CIRCUS

I just saw a handwritten note from
Galileo. He was under house arrest
for believing we're not the center of
everything. Now behind me, in the park,
a dozen beginners, of all ages, learning how
to juggle. We have to start somewhere. The
young man who's so magical at this is asked
to instruct. He smiles, "You have to keep
trying. Just not the same thing." Earlier,
I leaned over a letter from Lincoln to a
dead soldier's mother. This, just weeks
after losing Susan's mother, sweet
Eleanor. I keep saying her name to
strangers. You see, we all have to
juggle joy and sorrow. Not to do it
well—we always drop something—but
when the up and down of life are
leaving one hand and not yet land-
ing in the other, then we glow, like
a mystical molecule hovering between
birth and death, ready to kiss anything.

The Blood of Theology

He was insistent on framing
everything to his own way of thinking,
taking every effect and clipping it back
to the shape of his mind which like
a cookie cutter kept stamping
the things he saw,
the people he met,
the stories he heard.

For some reason,
I tried to make him understand.
I said, "The disease almost
took me from the Earth.
The rabid vehicle
almost crushed their daughter.
The alcohol in my brother's veins
almost made him bloodless."

He kept stamping around
with his cookie-cutter mind,
"Are you saying there is a God
or not?"

I sat with him and tried again:
"Sometimes, the weight of things
brings us to our knees, brings us
to a common pool in which
we're forced to see the underside
of what we show no one,

and in that moment, God
breaks our dearest principle
and we are left with the truth
of each other . . ."

He stopped to ponder this, and
I, unsure how such things build
in anyone, I felt the shadow of
a great bird enter him and then
through me, untying something
in us both.

INSEPARABLE

A small voice swept through the hole
in my heart, right there in the middle
of a day filled with the sweetness of
things outlasting our mistakes.

The voice led me to a thatch of
berries I had to eat, though the berries
were nested in a ring of thorns.

But this was the only food that
would heal. And everything I'd been
through, every path I'd tried, every love
I'd lost, every friendship I'd held onto like
a handle in a fire, every certainty that had
crumbled into doubt—all of it said,
"This is the only food."

The small voice whispered, "There
is no other way but to bury your face and
eat of these berries. Of course, you'll
scratch your cheeks. Of course, you'll
bleed. But this is life."

The berries nested in the thorns.
Inseparable as love nested in loss.
As peace nested in trouble.

Like God, waiting as a berry
to be eaten, all tangled
in the thorns.

My God, We Are Alive

For all the questions I've pressed the
wise with, for all the places I thought I
had to see, for all the birds I've envied
as they glide out of view, for all I keep
trying to hold up, though I've met those
I love over things I have dropped—the
moment I feel most tender is stepping
in the dark over slippers and books to
kiss you while you sleep. Once there,
I can't go on, or in, or out. I'm stalled
like a tear losing itself in the ocean.

Long Way Home

I want to have a conversation
that we can return to without
conclusion, one that lasts for
years, that feels like a walk that
has no end. Until the walk
itself is home.

I want to converse this life with
you, the way the old horse and
the young bird trudge and circle
each other in snow.

I want to reach with you into
the heart of things, where the
stitching of the Universe
shows its golden knots.

THE BOOK WON'T
LET ME HOLD IT

This morning, the sun spills
from the mountain to the page
and try as I will, I can't read the
poems; only the chiseled notes
in the back about their lives. This
one killed on a forced march to
Germany, his poems pulled from
a mass grave. Another began as a
basket weaver in Turin. And the
sad one who climbed the Sierra
Nevada in search of his dead wife.
And the old man from Shansi re-
turning for the early signs of spring.
Lifetimes to carry and carve what
no one can carry or carve. And
here the tender one whose only
crime was being sensitive. And
now, the lost one from the Sung
Dynasty who left only two poems,
like blue pebbles after a storm. Like
a waterfall gaining from its source,
spraying off the rocks below;
the lives of artists.

UNDERSTANDING
LEAVES

The leaves do what we can't.
They wait their whole lives.

At first they dream of air
and wait to slip from wood.

Then they dream of openness
and wait to stretch in light.

Then they dream of thirst
and wait to soften in the rain.

At last they dream of nothing
and simply unfurl.

Photosynthesis is how this waiting
is described in the physical world.

The mystery of waiting is what
turns light into food.

To wait beyond what we think
we can bear is how things
within turn sweet.

YES, WE CAN TALK

Having loved enough and lost enough,
I'm no longer searching
just opening,

no longer trying to make sense of pain
but trying to be a soft and sturdy home
in which real things can land.

These are the irritations
that rub into a pearl.

So we can talk for a while
but then we must listen,
the way rocks listen to the sea.

And we can churn at all that goes wrong
but then we must lay all distractions
down and water every living seed.

And yes, on nights like tonight
I too feel alone. But seldom do I
face it squarely enough
to see that it's a door
into the endless breath
that has no breather,
into the surf that human
shells call God.

INHABITING WONDER

If the sun thinks
by radiating light,
its language is warmth.

If the ocean thinks
by undulating its mass of waves,
its language is wetness.

If a tree thinks
by converting light to sugar,
its language
is the sprouting of leaves.

If the wind thinks
by moving unseen
through everything,
how it bends us
is its tongue.

I am tired
of only thinking like a man
and pray for the courage
to radiate, undulate, sprout,
and move through
everything
unseen.

THIS TIME

Funny how we love
in the way we want to be loved,
how we think of others in the way
we want to be thought of, how feeling
abandoned I vow never to abandon,
how being termed a disappointment
I slave not to disapprove, how finally
disappointment and disapproval
grow indiscernible as burns from
ice or heat, how now I'm up in the
night certain if I disappoint you
I am not worthy of your love, how
loving's become an obsession with
correcting the past, as if I'm strapped
to this rear-view mirror always looking
behind to move ahead, with this cramp
in my heart which I must hold till
it softens.

And when it softens, there will be
no waiting for you to speak first.
No more moping in that self-
mortared purgatory between
the feeling and the actual
living of it.

No, this time, I will take your hand
without hesitation as if you or I
are about to die, and if we live,

where our hands join, a flower
whose nectar will attract
even God.

This time, I will honor everything
including how rabbits chew
without looking at their food,
and how your aunt, now bedridden,
twists her hair as her mother did,
and how branches broken
stir the mud till flowers
split the gate.

This time,
I will enter the silence
in which my heart wakes, crisp
as the blue above God's wing.
This time, joy.

GOOD AS AIR

It's taken almost sixty years
but today as the wet grass
shines and the peaches soften,
I stand with nothing between
me and life. The dream I've
carried like a tent has come
down.

It wasn't a false dream, but a
plan I asked too much of. And
now it is complete. Not that I
arrived where I wanted or
achieved what I set out to
do. Just that it is finished.

Come. Look. As the sun
evaporates the rain that ripens
the peach, the dream, however
we personalize it, covers us
until we grow through it.

For the first time, I am
without covering. No map
or design or secret goal. It feels
good and unpredictable. Good
as air in the mouth of a turtle
shaking dirt from its eyes.

LETTING WHAT IS SHINE

I don't know Who—or what—put the question. I don't know when it was put. I don't even remember answering. But at some moment I did answer Yes to Someone—or Something—and from that hour I was certain that existence is meaningful and that, therefore, my life, in self-surrender, had a goal.

DAG HAMMARSKJÖLD

FEELING LOST

When I stop squirming, I realize
that lost is just an echo of where
I think I'm going or where
others think I should be.

When I cut the cord to the future
and the rope to the past, I have
trouble remembering what
makes me afraid.

With all the lines cut, I want
to spread before light like a young
tree and to do nothing.

Others are worried. When
I get more coffee, they whisper,
"He's lost his ambition." "He's lost
his focus." "He's getting old." But I
feel the coffee slip down my throat,
coaxing my voice to come alive.

A Nameless Ritual

You can, despite the innocence you were born
with, feel that something is missing, and try to
forget that you are empty, by reading hundred-
year-old novels, or planting dozens of bulbs, or
you can try to fix what you see as broken in others
until they call you kind, or you can look into the
hidden gears of the world until others think you
intelligent, and when nothing reaches you, you
can run into things until old ways crack, or you
can dive into your past till you catch what's been
eating at your heart, and once seizing it, you can
slowly and painfully bring it up until your fear
unfurls like a flag snapping and when all goes
limp, you might feel some spot of peace that's
been waiting beneath your name, and then you
can secretly feel the pain of wanting to be touched
by everything, and not being touched feel lost, and
being touched feel found, and not being touched
feel lonely, and being touched feel there might be
such a thing as joy, and then, something like a
quiet thirst might make you climb higher than all
obstacles until, with your arms to the wind, the
features you've been known by wear away and,
smelling the fumes of your birth, you might
risk that all thoughts are clouds and burn
them away with the heat of your being.

BELIEVING THE GUEST

Where do all the forgotten
promises land? "I would never
hurt you." "I will love you forever."
"What's mine is yours."

I have been on both sides.

Sometimes in our frailty
we don't follow through.
We simply don't deliver.
But often, we promise
what can't be promised.

It's not a matter of lying.
Though sometimes we lie.
More that the hawk's wings
can't cover the sky.

THE WORK
OF PRESENCE

When "I can't"
breaks down
into "Tell me who I am,"

When "I have no choice"
unravels
into "How can I help,"

When the tongue stuck in no
tires into yes,

the weight of everything
will explode into surprise,
and the pain of our knowing
will birth a love of strangers,
and the tools of tomorrow
will form safely
in the hearts
of our day.

When all we can do is freed
from all that has been done,
a presence that is everyone's
and no one's will keep
the inner time alive
the way the hearts
of young animals

beating while asleep
keep all the stars
in place.

AUTHORITY OF BEING

The sun doesn't stop shining
because some of us are blind.

The birds don't stop singing
because some of us are deaf.

The heart doesn't stop loving
because some of us are afraid.

What lets the flower in the forest
bloom though no one is watching?

A MIGHTY KINDNESS

Sometimes, though I'm not supposed
to know, I feel such a deep and timeless
ache that I'm certain my heart has
been alive for centuries.

Sometimes, it pulses with wounds and
joys that no one can withstand alone
and I go speechless.

In the actual moment of such feeling
I am a flag with no country

and in the days that follow
I often talk about freedom
and start to read many books,
never finishing them.

I start to write to friends
lost along the way
and stare at night
into lonelinesses
not entirely mine
and entirely mine.

My heart, though I'm not
supposed to know, is a red sun
holding me in its orbit.

But most precious
is how I feel

the timeless heart
in all things,
even in faceless grass,
waist high, and stone
glistening with frost, and in
you with the stars in your head.

Though I'm not supposed to know,
our lives flap like clothes on a line,
dancing to the movement of things
that can never be understood.

LETTING GO
OF THE NEED
TO BE LIKED

Bartering for affection
has come to an end.

I love you with no hope of
return like some inner sun
that has to spend its rays
or I lose my voice
like a singer hiding
in a hood.

If you love me back,
we will come alive.
If not, I will glimpse
the whole of life
by igniting my heart
like a match.

VIEW FROM THE HUT

The river carving the lip of the
mountain has always been, before
my father who never saw it, the clear
river grooving itself deeper into the
Earth, continually, forever, awaiting
my godchild's son, not yet born.

And the deer peering out of the dusk
to nibble the flowers so delicately planted,
yes, the planting and the nibbling have
gone on forever, too, as if one spirit
borrowing many lives has planted the
same flower over and over, so the one
spirit of deer borrowing the many lives
of deer could poke its head in the mist
to nibble the same soft colors again
and again.

And the want to be loved, repeated in-
finitely the way little sea creatures suck
at the bottom when the current slows,
only to be thrown about when the current
picks up, only to suck at a new bottom
when the current slows and on and on.
From the eye of God, the whole of hu-
manity pulses as tiny, vibrant life forms
living off each other in the deep.

It's all gone on forever and it's humbling
and freeing on this rainy May morning

to realize that my heart which seems, at
times, so vast a pit of feeling that I fear
I'll never stand firmly on its rim, to
realize that this agitated canyon in
which I live is just a pinhole
to the Mysteries.

TOSSED ABOUT

It's only been two weeks and
already I've had to tell your story
to someone who never knew you.

And yesterday, a friend gave birth
and I wonder if that child is you
without the details or is this
my refusal to let you go?

A shock of geese winging
overhead seems to answer:
it's more than one to one.

Can it be that life exposes and
covers us like surf, tossing us
about, moving grains of soul like
sand from one shell to the next?

On the radio, a young voice
croons a song made famous by
someone long gone, written by
another whose name we'll
never know. Already I've had
to stop and tell your story.

THE PRAYER
OF RESISTANCE

I'm no longer surprised
to look up and see others,
beautiful tired others,
climbing or descending
alongside me.

All of us building
our way out of pain
or fleeing the exquisite
trapeze of our dreams.

All this scurrying for deep
serious purpose, only to find
a little bench from which
to glimpse the unseeable
wave of everything.

And all along
it's been God's trick
to dissolve what we want
like rice in rain until
exhaustion is the prayer
against our will
that drops us
into peace.

BREAKING
ALL PRINCIPLE

Left in the open,
I settle like a rock
waiting for the sea,
to endure a knowledge
I sorely need.

Left in the open,
my thoughts are washed
like footprints in surf, and
my understanding, far from
being destroyed, becomes
uncluttered.

Left in the open,
I feel the beginning where
I was touched alive, before
tongue had word and mind
had thought.

There burns the fire
I was born with, the
fire that conveys me.

THE QUARTER TURN

I suddenly knew I was looking at it from
the wrong angle and I gave the cloth in my
hand a quarter turn. Immediately I saw a
beautiful and coherent golden pattern . . .
In wonder, the pattern had emerged, to be seen
in all its beauty by those who could learn to
make the quarter turn.
                              HELEN LUKE

When six I'd watch frogs and
squirrels and lots of little birds:
sparrow, titmouse, chickadee.
Something in how they
moved seemed a secret.

Once I chased a butterfly
halfway through the reservoir
before cupping it in my boyish
hands. I had the beautiful thing,
but couldn't see it. To see it,
I had to let it go.

I kept my hands cupped as long as
I could, past nose itch and leg jiggle,
and then the dark flitting against my
palms made me open, and magnificent
plates of color lifted against my will.
It was too delicate a story to tell over
dinner and soon there were books

and assignments and model cars
to glue and arguments and anger
and I forgot.

It's only now, forty years later,
that it awakens me.

Now it seems a way of life:
afraid to lose, we chase and cling,
and clinging, we are lost.

It seems so obvious once seen;
like the face of God discovered
in stone, never just stone
again.

Oh what we feel beats darkly
within, only uplifting
the instant we let go.

STACKS OF WHEAT

So many thought Monet
was making it up,
imagining wildly
how things might be
if God held them closer.

But what he did
was much braver.
Like a human microscope
he kept looking and looking
as warmth left the trees
as waves remade the sea
as loss slowed into peace
undoing hard men.

He watched
strange flowers open
where only silence had been.

He focused so far in
that everything shimmered.
He proved by the strength
of his attention that
nothing can keep
light out.

It's a small leap
to say that love
works this way—

a light that lives in the bones,
just waiting to be seen.

So why not
prop your heart
out in the open
like the easel that it is
and dab its blood
on everything.

DREAMS OF JOY

It could be someone
you never had the courage
to love, holding you
in the night.

Or talking all night
with a lifelong friend,
both of you lucid and hungry,
the talk peeling, not adding up,
but peeling into uncontrollable
laughter and the smell
of honey.

It could be swimming
deeper than ever, alongside
iridescent fish, copying
their wriggle for light.

Or taking something apart so
thoroughly—a car, a watch—that
it never has to be put together
again, and you, caught in the
joy of the thing dismantled.

It could be righting a turtle
and watching it stare at you
before receding in its shell.

Or righting yourself
and staring at the world.

THE RHYTHM OF EACH

I think each comfort—each holding
in the night, each opening of a wound,
each closing of a wound, each pulling
of a splinter or razored word, each
fever sponged, each dear thing given
to someone in greater need—each
passes on the kindness we have known.

For the human sea is made of cares
that mount and merge till the way a
nurse rocks a child is the way that child
all grown rocks the wounded, and how
the wounded, allowed to go on, can
rock strangers free of their pain.

Eventually, the rhythm of kindness
is how we suffer and pray by turns,
and if someone were to watch us
from inside the lake of time, they
wouldn't be able to tell if we are
dying or being born.

OLD WINDOW

There are days like today
when the God within creaks
me open like an old window
shut too long. And before I
get cold, before it rains, before
I realize I am open and rush
to close myself, a bee wanders
in. I'm immediately afraid
of being stung. But
what if it's God's bee
come to pollinate me?

ECLIPSE OF LOVE

To say that the bridge gave way
and killed the boy weeding the bank—
when that is what happened—
is a brave bit of being.

To admit that you hid
from the glass breaking in
the next room—that you hummed
anything to drown out the yelling—
is a brave bit of truth.

To honor that the first breath
after pain can eclipse
what is cruel is a courage
that can save us.

Sometimes faith
is moaning like a wounded
animal no matter who is around.
And singing what is true can
heal others without their knowing.

OVER COFFEE

This morning it's raining,
gently, while my wife is sleeping,
our dog curled in my space.

And for some reason, I've fallen
into the quiet basin of my heart
where all my loves mix. In there,
the friends and lovers and strangers
and the family I no longer talk to—
in there, they've softened like
cardboard floating in the ocean.

The light rain at the window is
saying, "Don't. Don't think too
hard—just drift."

Can it be—that all our lives we're
just funny shaped cups and mugs:
sometimes clear, sometimes not,
sometimes chipped, sometimes
too hot to hold?

Can it be—the whole sorry struggle
for a self is just to have something
sturdy enough to carry the love?

MUSIC TO READ WIND BY

When I decide I love you just as you've
left town, when you muster the courage
to forgive your father and go to say so
only to find he's had a stroke, and you
never know what he hears as I never
know where you are, when I hold my
face to the wind and my questions dis-
appear—it's the music of near misses that
lets me know that my heart is just a reed.

In the realm of things so large and silent
we sometimes think we're all there is, no-
thing should surprise us. And given enough
time, the dark will tear into light and the
children of enemies will run off to sire a
softer world and the fire of their love
will burn the records of revenge.

Sometimes the clap of a single heart
can change the politics of worth, can
make the thief bow down and plant
what he's stolen, or let us wounded lovers
sigh, believing for an instant that our
capacity to feel is the blood that stirs time.

Sometimes to speak, not knowing what,
save that it comes from a well older
than all shame, sometimes this sort
of truth can rearrange the stars.

153

LETTING WHAT IS SHINE

Perhaps the greatest addiction
is self-centeredness: living like
a piece of dark making everything dark,
like an inch of me making everything me.

You may be thinking, "Well, this isn't good.
I do this sometimes." We all do. But love
and disappointment like rain can cleanse
us, if we don't hide from them.

The practice, when hearing another's
pain, is to somehow hold it, like
a broken star, a bleeding star,
in the middle of your chest,
just for a moment, without
pairing it with your own.

DISROBING IN TIME

Nothing is easy, but to tell the truth.
The truth of what I see and feel.
This somehow cleanses my eye
and it becomes clear what to do.

In my pain I forget to admit what is
true and things get worse. Because
I don't want to be sad, I don't admit
that I already am. Then I feel like
I'm drowning.

Because I don't want things to change,
I don't admit that they already have.
Then I feel like the wheel of life
is tearing me apart.

The greatest power we have when
feeling powerless is to admit what
is already true. Then the stepping
stones of Eternity rise out of the
mud, showing us where to go.

NOW THAT I FEEL

how little time there is, I'm
falling in love with everything:
the stranger whose name I'll
never know, and the crow
pecking at the half bagel
she left for him.

Now that the walls I didn't
know were walls have come
down, I want to care for
everything. And the sun
warming in all directions
without preference is
showing me how.

Today my heart aches,
not because something is
lacking, but because the love
I've carried all along is bursting
through all the gates of choice.

Signs of the One Essence

The tops of clouds that no one sees
illuminated by the sun.

The inside of the heart that no one sees
softened by the soul.

The calm waiting at the center
of all silence.

The warmth waiting at the center
of all feeling.

The coolness waiting at the bottom
of a lake.

The emptiness waiting at the bottom
of all ideas.

The first sign of light that stirs
birds to sing.

The wordless beginning that awakens
the encumbered.

Understanding is only the movement
between seasons.

In

This head is a big jar put down over a lantern.
RUMI

IN

The Mystery needs
authentic souls to bear
witness to it, the way
matter needs atoms to
hold it together, the way
blood needs cells to keep
it alive. So I no longer ask
why but how. Not the
mechanical how. But how
to stand on nothing like
an atom in the center
that is everywhere.

IN THE MILKY OCEAN

As you pour milk on your cereal, I am
grateful for the sound of milk flowing over
dried grain, for the peace that lets us wake
and eat together, to stare at each other in
silence like small animals. I am aware how
safely tumbled through Eternity we are. Not
to be hunted from birth. Or chased into the
forest and forced to part. Or beaten for a
secret some warlord thinks we're hiding. I
eat my toast and close my eyes. How is it
we're alive in a place that has running water,
where milk and eggs are plentiful? Atrocities
and wonders flutter through me. They bleed
into each other. I can't stop it. The milk
tastes good as my twin is somewhere on
the run. It seems impossible to feel so
many fates at once. Impossible not to.

In the Spaces

Even as a teenager, when left
by my buddies on a night beach,
the heavens opened their ancient
hollow and I wandered in the
safety of wordless spaces.

Though we have to return to
the world, the ground of being
waits in the glint of brick and
the steam rising through
an open window.

I'm thankful that life has
broken my impatience
beyond repair.

INTUITION

We think if we want some-
thing bad enough, our guess
will become our destination.

It's how we bend the Universe
to our will for an instant.

But I need a horse who given
the chance will follow life.

It takes a greater will to sit
so lightly that the horse will
gallop as if it has no rider.

INTO THE NEXT LIFE

I lived for so long, wings spread,
catching high currents, that when
God sent me on by holding his
breath, I thought I was failing,
missing what carried me, and so
I tried harder, but just kept dropping,
afraid I was losing myself. And I was.
Against my will, I spiraled down till
all flapping was useless. I was certain
I was falling to my death, though I
was only being brought closer to
the Earth. Closer to the secret
that is never really secret. Till
I could land in who I am.

SOFTER THAN TRUTH

You may have expected that enlightenment would come like zap!
Instantaneous and permanent. This is unlikely. After the first
"aha," it can be thought of as the thinning of a layer of clouds.

RAM DASS

The ocean refuses no river.

RUMI

THE TRUTH
OF EXPERIENCE

Imagine a river of fire
and you are a piece of wood
in which someone has hidden
a jewel and no matter how you
try, you are destined to burn your
way to the falls where just when
you feel certain you will die, the
weight of the wood burns off
and only the jewel floats over the
edge and the pool at the bottom
cleanses what has been hidden for
so long. Beyond the fall, the deep
is what's been waiting under
the fire and the jewel is what's
been waiting under the wood
and the air praises what
has never been seen.

GREAT UNSEEABLE THUNDERS

We drive over an hour and before the recital,
there's only one waitress. We have to wait and
the lamb is overcooked. Finally, the pianist born
in St. Petersburg begins to play a fugue from Bach
who fathered twenty children. Someone murmurs,
he should have kept it in his pants, as two old hens
keep fumbling through their bags. Then the fugue
in F unravels me. The music works its honeyed
smoke till a slender woman drops her head, all
slouch and throw of sorrow, as if to say, alright, I
see it, too. The underside of life is throbbing every-
where. During Chopin's nocturne, a boy lays his
head on the table, opening his eyes to all he is
to live, as his sister stares into the immensity of
time, keeping herself here by the run of her fingers
through her baby brother's hair. Now our puppet
strings are cut and everyone's drifting in the vast-
ness, though no one can look there long. The
great loneliness is apparent in the older woman's
face as she lays down her purse like a heavy shield.
And the man with suspenders, who was a pain in
the ass at dinner, is looking for his wife who died
so long ago, and the father of three realizes that
all he's ever wanted is right before him as he eyes
these large flowers which everyone says are his
daughters. And the great flurry of the pianist's

hands levels all attitude the way a powerful surf
breaks ridges of sand. We forget what really
matters till someone driven to center makes it
cry out. It takes an avalanche of tragedy or
a whisper of grace to make us admit
we are more than our fear.

THE DESCENT

How do we live in a world
where all things are true?
Yet we do. Like a pebble
tossed in the ocean, each
soul dropped into the world
floats slowly—though to us
it seems so fast—while a thou-
sand things come together, tear
apart, prey on each other, grow
from the bottom, leap for the
light, and scatter from sudden
disturbance. All the while, the
soul drifts lower and we resist
the drift and trouble ourselves
about purpose and where we're
headed and if we're thrown off
course. But there's nothing more
quietly beautiful than a soul
entering the sea of existence,
finding its place below
all the noise.

SOFTER THAN TRUTH

They say, after thousands of seasons,
the Great Spirit grew weary of being
all-knowing by itself, and so caused
us to love, that we might sweep
behind each other's eyes.

They say what we remember of
a dream is the kiss of the Great
Spirit quenching its loneliness.

They say when we see through
the eyes of another, the Great
Spirit is stitching our hearts
to hold the world together.

WANTING MOMENTS

In one gesture, the entire Chi. In
one image escaping the heart, the
entire poem. In one kiss that we pour
ourselves into, the vastness we all share.
A thousand names and none quite do
it. Getting wet completely, once, holds
the secret of the ocean.

THE DIVE

Brave your way on.
You are a blessing waiting
to be discovered by yourself.
The wisdom waits in your heart
like a buried treasure which
only loving your self can
bring to the surface. And
yes, loving your self is like
diving to the bottom of the
ocean with nothing but who
you are to find your way.

HEARTSONG

In the darkness I'm
always surprised to revisit,
I know that somewhere
the light keeps dripping
honey on my wounds.

And just when I can't
bear to hear another story,
I realize my song has
hidden for a while
inside the truth of others.

Now I must ask and listen
again. Each of us hacking
through the forest that
grows over the heart.

Just when about to give
up, the world prods my
sorry head into the bird
it wants to be.

THE DEEPER CHANCE

Mira is our dog-child.
And though we held her as a pup,
she has a need to be held
that comes from beyond us.
Though I sat with her when
she was the size of a loaf of bread,
sat on the kitchen floor staring softly
into her eyes, she has a need to stare
that comes from a place beneath
the awkwardness of humans.

These days, she seems a furry naked
thing that never looks away.

Now, I understand: God made the animals
as raw breathing elements, each closer
in their way to one aspect of being.

And that the friction of time on Earth
might have its chance to make us wise,
God made the animals speechless.

We've learned that Mira in Spanish
means to look. And lately, she licks us
awake and stares deep into us, as if to say,
Get up. Don't look away. Admit
you need to be held.

No More Crisis
to Hero Through

I have no reason anymore
to be other than I am.

The things that grow into soul,
though they depend on everything,
need no one's approval.

And the love I've wanted so badly
softens in the patches of ground
showing through the snow.

We humans have misconstrued the
way. Beauty is not just to look at—it is
food and those destined to find their
beauty are also destined to be used.

In time, we feed off each other and,
though we can taint everything with
our fear, we can be battered from our
grip until we take turns being that
which wants and that which is
found, taking lifetimes to be
the patch of light or the vine
inching out the ground.

FALLING THROUGH

I have fallen through,
and though it felt like dying,
once below, I saw the bottom
of things lighted from above
and this has made the difference.

Of course, this is not the end of it.
Like Sisyphus or Prometheus,
each day re-enacts the whole thing.

Each day, I wrestle with waves
of doubt and fear and recurring
blindnesses, and then, if I suffer
or love enough, I fall through
and die to my undoing again,
to where it's holy to be silent
and adrift, and there I see the
belly of all fear lighted from
above.

And this makes you and me
and the stranger we avoid
shine like the flawed beings
we are.

It makes me leave the house
unlocked and enter the world
full of praise. It makes me
reach through the fire
in reckless song.

ATTEMPTS

When the old life is
burning, everything will
smell like ash for a while.
So trust your heart,
not your nose.

Trust the music of the
ages to surface what's left
way inside. Wait like a
cello for each rub to
bring you closer.

Learn how to ask for
what you need, only to
practice accepting what
you're given. This is our
journey on Earth.

For the Thousandth Time
I Want to Know

If an empty box
is torn apart, the air
inside still joins the rest.

If an empty heart is
shattered, the love inside
still coats the stars.

And when a dove is born,
its shell is done.

How much fear we know
depends on whether we live
as something torn apart
or as the air released.

How much pain turns to
suffering depends on whether
we live as something shattered
or as the love about to join.

We can live as a shell
waiting to crack or as a
dove waking to its song.

A FUGITIVE AWARENESS

[When] I have to cross a large open
space I forget everything.

This is the purpose of large open
spaces—like the eyes of someone
you're about to love—to make
you forget the things you
weren't born with.

At birth there are two unfoldings
which no one can escape: the
path from trouble to all we
have to face, and the path
from stillness to grace.

Sooner or later, we come to the
edge of a vastness that has been
there all along and we are forced
to decide if we are visitors
or if this is our home.

How the Divine Speaks

I tried to think about my problem
but the wind from behind a cloud
brushed the thought from my face
and my worry entered the crow on
the roof who started to caw. Then
the crow coughed up my worry and
began to fly. We can't caw and fly
at the same time. I never noticed
this. Look. Now the wild grass is
bowing to be coated by the light.
If I could only learn to bow.

THE SECOND FLOWER

She was stopped by the light on a peony
on the north side of the city. A few days
later, she saw another peony in her friend's
yard. But she thought, I've seen this flower
before. And so, she didn't pay attention.

But it was the second flower
that held a secret for her.

Pretty soon, she thought life was
repeating, when all that was repeating
was her want for a flower she'd never seen.

WHY ALL THE NOISE?

So what is it we want?

When holding out,
I suffer such loneliness.

And you, afraid of the real,
hide inside your life, hoping
no one will find you.

Let's be honest, we both
take turns. When hurt,
we run like fugitives
from the spokes of the world.

When I can stop,
it appears to me briefly
that life is just a dance
around a still point, which
knowing is a joy and
refusing is a burden.

So why all the noise?
We can't escape the journey
or undo it, anymore than
the Earth can undo its orbit.

Experience will point us to Spirit,
the way water swirls around a center
that has no water, the way God who

has no face draws all faces
into the Mystery.

ONTOLOGY

What I think matters less
than what comes through me.
What does a flag really know
of the wind? Or a bee of the
pollen it carries? Or a soul
of its maker?

THE STRIPPING OF OUR WILL

Like the silk that keeps the corn shiny,
all our delicate dreams
have served their purpose
once the heart pops up
like a kernel.

Now there is only
the chance to be sweet.

So dream as you will, plan
to build your version of the pyramids.
Scheme to make and spend several fortunes.

Nothing matters but the sweetness,
the sweetness incubated
in our dreams and sufferings,
finally husked and
brought to air.

AS WE MOVE DEEPER

into this mysterious river, I pray
we don't turn every thing
we touch into us,

that we help each other listen more
deeply than we have ever listened,

that we baptize each other
with what we find there

that we heal each other's
blindnesses by pouring love like
water on each other's eyes

and that waking in this way,
we make the unseen breath of God
visible, the way wind can only lift
a tree that has grown in the open.

STAYING AWAKE

If you can, have a loved one
draw your bath. If you're alone,
be your own loved one. Make sure
the water won't burn but is just
hotter than you think you can bear.
Have a candle nearby, a small flame
to remind you of the wordless voice
that is in everything. As you slip in,
remember there is nothing between
you and life. If you can, use a sponge,
one from the sea, and hold it under
till it's filled with warmth. Now look
at the sponge as if meeting it, and as
it streams on your hands bruised
from the day, listen for its story:
how it grew in place, rooted gently
in the deep, how its only purpose
is to absorb and stream, how its
story is your story. You are holding
yourself. So hold yourself under and
let the warmth stream over your head
so tired of its plotting and solving, let
it stream over your eyes so tired of all
this seeing, and over your mouth so tired
of searching for the end of all speech, and
over your ears so tired of not hearing. Finally,
squeeze the sponge over your heart that aches
to be a sponge. And close your eyes till your
whole body is an eye that hears the Oneness

in things. Now you can see how the water
registers the slightest movement of your
breath, how it soothes you without keep-
ing or losing any of itself. Now you can
imagine that this is how we love
when the heart is a sponge. And
once you've lost all sense of time,
let the water drain around you.
Do not move. Just let the water
recede and feel the coolness of
the air refind your skin. Now
towel and dress and go back
into the world, saying nothing
of this, but with your eyes.

TO WEAR LIGHT

Lately,
there is more space
around my words
and I suspect what is true
waits between
the utterance
and its echo.

If you look here,
the way you might
follow a thread of sun
through a break in the
undergrowth,
I think you'll
understand.

Like Lazarus
I am calm
only because
I've already died

and this life after life
is so ordinary
it is raw.

Touch me
when I am fully here
and we just might ignite
into a faceless joy.

COVENANT OF WIND

I have heard long secrets trapped in the
Earth and I fear none of it, only the inability
to recall what one friend did for another,
what one depth did to its shore. I have
found this spot high above the surf
where gulls glide the drafts. They ride
at eye level. They warn me that the world
is full of those who when cold take more
than they give. In the wind below, wet
dogs run the surf chasing pipers, and
barely recognizable human forms let
their legs sink like roots, as children
throw bottles and rocks at anything
they see moving from the sea. And
now they're running to the top and
jumping to roll the soft landslide, then
climbing back. I've always known it. Before
I had eyes to collect evidence of pain, before
I had arms to feel for a way: to climb, to see,
and fall. This is the covenant. And given
the chance to run the shores of the world,
I would change nothing but the fate of legs
and hearts to be born strong. I have been
dark and bewildered much of the time.
But when I have seen like today a power
in the steadfast pose of stone upon stone
closest to the sky, when I have felt the
wind after lifetimes round my teeth and
make a singing cavern of my head, I

have, briefly, enough love to carry
the world around again.

BOOK THREE

THE WAY UNDER THE WAY

*Like a traveler who
sheds his bundles as
he tires, the dream of
life I so wanted weighed
me down, until living
my life led me to bare
the dream and be
the dream*

THE PLACE OF TRUE MEETING

The young British poet John Keats said, "Heard melodies are sweet, but those unheard are sweeter." More than the music of silence, I think Keats, who was dying of tuberculosis, was pointing to the music of life that plays continuously just below our normal hearing. Over the years, I've learned that moments of deep living—brought about by unexpected doses of love, suffering, loss, beauty, or truth—let us hear this deeper music, if all too briefly. Yet it's this timeless terrain that brings us alive. We can call this foundational geography, the way under the way.

It's always been true that beneath the curl of every wave, an anonymous force of life shoulders the depth of all there is, making that wave swell. And beyond the rustle of every tree, a long, forgotten wind rises quietly from the endless basin of time. And behind every blessing we can't explain, an unseen element brings us together when we're too exhausted to resist. Everything visible rises out of a greater, invisible force that brings it into being. Under every act of courage or love, there's a momentum of braveries and care that has gathered and passed through everyone who ever lived. The third book in this collection explores that place of true meeting which is always near.

When the hardships of living make us forget that there is more to life than our hardships, poetry—as a way of being, feeling, and perceiving—returns us to the way under the way. To our constant surprise, enduring our hardships—which involves opening our pain and fear and loss, rather than sealing them over—is how we drink from the waters of life.

The sections here explore how opening and closing are natural rhythms to living, which if treated as an art can keep us vital. In the section "The Practice Before the Practice," the poems examine how inhabiting the ground of being prepares us for living in the world. In the section "A Thousand Stories On," the poems praise how all our stories are threads in the one unending story and how honoring this gives us strength. And in the section "The End of All Striving," the poems speak to the acceptance that all we ever need is right where we are, if we can open the ordinary treasure that is always before us.

It's archetypal that we all try to distinguish ourselves in the first half of life, trying to find our unique gift and contribution, trying to discover how special, different, and extraordinary we are. But eventually, we're transformed by experience to seek what we have in common with all life, so we might discover our one true kinship. This shift from trying to be special to seeking what is special in everything marks the way under the way.

By its very nature, what keeps us alive defies being named, though I keep trying. Like a whale compelled to break surface in order to breathe, like a whale compelled to go back into the deep to live in its element   how alive we truly are depends on the way under the way.

FOUND AND CLEARED

Each poem has been a path,
found and cleared, to the same hill
under the stars where I have met
everyone who ever lived.

There, dreams as they fall
turn into fish and pains as
they rise turn into birds.

There, when I still my
tongue and rest my mind,
each wound of the world
becomes a star too bright
to stare into, too hot to touch.

Though no one can live there,
that hill is necessary like the sun.

You want to call it God.
There are many names.
I call it a gift.

THE PRACTICE
BEFORE THE PRACTICE

The first word, "Ah," blossoms into all others.
Each of them is true.

KUKAI

BEING HERE

Transcending down into
the ground of things is akin
to sweeping the leaves that
cover a path. There will always
be more leaves. And the heart
of the journey, the heart of our
awakening, is to discover for
ourselves that the leaves are not
the ground, and that sweeping
them aside will reveal a path,
and finally, that to fully live,
we must take the path and
keep sweeping it.

NOT ACCORDING TO PLAN

When I drop my glasses
in the airport and they're
crushed in the walkway
between terminals, I get to
meet the three kind souls
who help me on my way.

Then I hear you crying
after everyone has left.
So I bring you water
and hear your story.

Ever since the lock on
my door broke, I have
more visitors.

Now the road I always
take is detoured, which
I curse until I see the
heron glide across the
small pond I didn't
know was there.

THIS I KNOW

I don't know which I love more:
The moment before I feel your lips
or the ache when I remember we are
here with nothing between us.

I don't know which helps more:
The stars in their steadiness or the
dark that makes them shine. I don't
wish for storms, but I'm in awe how
the soul is worn to its shine in their
turmoil. How I love the exhaustion
of being tossed about till we drop
our masks.

I don't know which I need more:
The drift of not knowing or the
breathlessness of understanding.

Don't know which is the greater
teacher: The lift of dreams that shape
the world or the majesty of things
as they are.

But to kick off the covers without
waking you, to let the dog out
and breathe in the stars while
the coffee drips—this I know,
the way grass gives in
to its love of weather.

BELOW OUR
STRANGENESS

My soul tells me, we were
all broken from the same name-
less heart, and everything wakes
with a piece of that original heart
aching its way into blossom. This
is why we know each other below
our strangeness, why when we fall,
we lift each other, or when in pain,
we hold each other, why sudden
with joy, we dance together. Life
is the many pieces of that great
heart loving itself back together.

In Singing
the Secrets

How do wingless birds
fly? They move around in
the same place and think of
the sky. Some say this was
the origin of dance.

And how do you know
if someone loves you?
When they commit to
your growth and not to
your staying the same.

What is the purpose
of a name, if not to be
washed away by love?

So when I say I love you—
not like a greeting, but like
a confession at the end of
a long journey which makes
me realize that everything I
thought secret is only of
use if sung—I am saying
that I will give up my
name for your growth.

THESE HUMAN DAYS

As the fog lifted, we sat on the couch,
our dog sleeping between us, her fur
with that smell of rain. Our hands
met in the tuft of her neck. Later,
after a very bad movie, we fell into
each other for the thousandth time.
I thought, how seldom we are naked.
No veils or coverings. Your lips were
soft. They're always soft. And in that
softness, it's unclear where I end and
you begin.

Today I'm in the dentist chair, deep
long drilling around old nerves. Five
shots to numb along the bone. As he
drills, I loft into his eyes. He's such a
good man. The dog, your lips, his kind
eyes, the fog lifting. I start to tear.
Such a privilege to feel.

Now I'm in the car and the rain is
coaxing the grass on the side of the
road. My jaw aches and what wants
to be said waits under that ache. The
longer this goes, the stronger and more
vulnerable I am. Like two blades
of grass splitting the sidewalk.

ATTENDANT SPIRITS

The angels around us, the ones
I've seen when too tired to think,
the one who twitches in our dog
when she sleeps, the one who rides
the sun through the fork in the oak,
the one who weighs the angry hand
open, the one who like a breeze lifts
the curtain of my eyes, the one who
flits like a dragonfly in the back of
my throat telling me it's ok to cry—
they don't come to help us *out* of
here. They quietly wait for the
storms of paradise to crack, for
the dreams we lean on to topple.
They soak up light and wait like
dew on grass for us to notice—
then slip in through our
smallest sigh.

FLIGHT STATUS

We pack, we go, we shimmy
through a few tight places,
tell a few stories, and land.
We unpack. Each time
we pack a little less.

We cover ourselves
in brief histories, another
kind of baggage, and shimmy
through circumstances that
make us drop things
along the way.

We lose our story.
We find another.
We change our name.
We pack even less.

And so, on this day,
when you have lost your way,
I want to congratulate you
and give you something
of mine, before I lose it
or it's broken in the dark.

A small something you can
hold onto, as you are worn
to who you were born to be.

Our names change.
Our histories fall away.
Our stories tell themselves.

What's left is what matters.
It's where this has been going.

Loose Like Silk

The other night at dinner
Eileen tells us that her great
aunt played piano for silent
movies. Something in this won't
let me go. Perhaps it's the thought
of someone playing music in the
dark while we watch others, like
us, meet life in silence. It makes
me think of a caveman drumming
a stone with a stick while his brother
draws his bow but fails to shoot be-
cause he loses himself in the bison
grazing. Perhaps the playing of
images in the dark and the play-
ing of music while we watch is all
to keep us from shooting. I think
the brother who loses himself and
Eileen's aunt playing Brahms in the
dark are of the same tribe. Last night
we went next door for a glass of wine
with Stacy and Anders, and their blind
collie Kai broke my heart open a little
further. He noses gently toward every-
thing and watching him find his way
about the yard in the late sun feels
like you and me when we admit we
haven't a clue. Kai's soft, wide eyes
search in their darkness for the shelf
of late light and finding something,

he rests his head in the open air, in
the warm hand of Eternity, feeling
safe in a light he can't see.

LISTENING TO CLOUDS

I've outlived the myth that love
is reserved for people, saved for
lovers or those of the same blood.

I've suffered my way into the open where
love like light enlivens everything, including
the stone in my shoe that makes me stop
and sit in the grass which I have forgotten.

From there, the low wind which I seldom
feel makes my eyes water. That brings our
dog to lick my face. And that brings you till
we're all lying in the grass looking at the
clouds drifting out of the way. Then, you
take my hand and sigh, "This is Heaven."

THE GIVERS

When the doctors broke their huddle,
her uncle leaned in, "What would you like?"
The little girl beamed, "A white piano!"
It took him three weeks but he had
one waiting in her room. She played
it every day like the medicine it was.

And the guitar player stopping for water
in Virginia, hearing the gas station owner
on the phone, "I got no choice. I gotta put
'em down." The young man keeps telling
everyone, "I don't know why, but I had
to take them." Now the old dog and
her pups live in his car.

And the nurse who dreams of her
grandma in the backseat on long trips
warming her little girl hands. And the
cashier, in awe of her sister who after ten
years of meditating gave it up to care for
orphans. Not 'cause she was done with it,
but 'cause what she found there is now
everywhere.

And the therapist who opens the memory
of her father like an old napkin holding a
pressed flower. A country doctor, he took
chickens instead of money. She was thirteen
when he died. After the funeral, her brother,

in a burst of grief, dumped her father's books
in the burning barrel. It began to rain and the
books, like broken doves, just softened and
enlarged. When everyone left, she gathered
them up. Now when it rains, she
opens one and he talks to her.

And the son of a heroin addict
serving soup in a shelter, thinking, as
he pours the ladle a hundred times a day,
"The givers seldom know what they give."

THE MYTH OF URGENCY

Everyone wants you to quietly be Atlas,
to shoulder it all. Even the voice in your
head insists you are behind. But I've seen
the light in you, the one the gods finger
while we sleep. I've seen the blossom open
in your heart, no matter what remains to
be done. There are never enough hours
to satisfy the minions of want. So close
your eyes and lean into the Oneness that
asks nothing of you. When the calls stack,
answer to no one, though you receive them
all. Just open your beautiful hands, born with
nothing in them. You have never been more
complete than in this incomplete moment.

I SHOUT THEIR NAMES

I'm at an age where those I've known
for years are dying. Some go quick, like
snow on a warm day. Some more slowly,
as if every week is a tide that takes them
farther and farther away.

To lose someone you love is to be
seized by an invisible hand that pulls
a clump of earth from your heart.

Only after months is it possible to
know that there is more room to feel.

Now I see your faces in the knots of
trees and chase leaves because I some-
how think they hold things you
meant to say. Now I cry at garlic
bread because you loved its smell.

Perhaps this is your gift to us:
to take up space so far in that
when you go, you empty us out.

And in our grief, we look for you
everywhere till against our will
we rediscover the world.

THINKING LIKE
A BUTTERFLY

Monday I was told I was good.
I felt relieved.
Tuesday I was ignored.
I felt invisible.
Wednesday I was snapped at.
I began to doubt myself.
On Thursday I was rejected.
Now I was afraid.
On Saturday I was thanked
for being me. My soul relaxed.
On Sunday I was left alone
till the part of me that can't
be influenced grew tired of
submitting and resisting.
Monday I was told I was good.
By Tuesday I got off the wheel.

YOU ASK
ABOUT POETRY

You ask from an island
so remote it remains un-
spoiled. And four thousand
miles away, as the sun ices the
snow, I smile. For to search for
stones on a beach holds something
of the way. After years of looking,
I can only say that to walk quietly
till the miracle in everything speaks
is poetry. And to search for small
things worn by the deep is to be
a poet. But to listen to what
they say is to be the poem.

PHYSICS OF THE DEEP

I'm a big, old fish now, gumming
at the bottom, happy to feel the
light dissolve around me like sugar.
Each of our lives unfolds this way,
all that we touch dissolving over time
into a sweetness. Each of us: a hard-
ness carrying a softness, a determina-
tion carrying a gift, a thickness carry-
ing fruit. It's hard to bear. And so, we
run into experience and each other:
to crack our hardness, to break our
determination, to get through our
thickness. Each of us destined to
shatter the container we live in,
so the sweetness can escape.

THE MYSTIC SPINNING
OF THREADS

I wonder where you are tonight.
Each of you. You who I lived with
for twenty years. You who I grew
up with. You who I almost loved.

Are you searching for a sweater
as the sun goes down? Are you
running from the law? Or from
yourself as we did so long ago?

I feel you dancing with each other
in the basement of my heart. When
I call, you hush each other till I'm
drawn into some other trouble.

I hope you're not plagued with
regret. Some things are not meant
to mend, but break into some-
thing entirely life altering.

We did what we could.

BREAKING BREAD

The giver is used up in the giving
as rain evaporates in what it helps
to grow. It's human to fear this, but
we can no more resist it than the pit
can resist becoming fruit.

When you help me up, you absorb
part of my fall. But somehow it
doesn't make you fall.

This is the inoculation of love.

The giver is remade in the giving
the way wax is remade in every flame.

Anything That Glistens

How do trees deal with injustice?
They grow a branch wherever they are cut.
And how do sparrows deal with grief?
They open their tiny wings and swoop
at anything that glistens.

So, why am I all cut and hungry?

Because I don't know the tree
that is my soul and
refuse the sparrow
in my heart.

HEARTWORK

The simple ways are hardest to see
because they are so close. Like seeing
your palms while digging in the earth.
Or seeing your eyes while looking
at the moon. Or seeing the
truth when utterly afraid.

We think what we need is so
far away. Yet it's as close
as ocean to fish.

It's all so simple. And so hard.
As listening without hope of reward,
the way mountains listen to the sun.
Or holding nothing back, the way
rivers can't stop flowing to the sea.

Simple as snow on the tongue
of a child. Yes, God appears
like that.

BAREBACK

No question I've been
knocked from my horse.
And the one with tools
in his hands keeps prodding:
Get back in the saddle. What are
you waiting for? But the timeless
one affirms: *You're not listening.*
There is no more saddle. We've done
away with all that. The driven one
keeps looking at his watch: *You*
didn't work all these years to walk
away now. But the one who
breathes like a flower replies:
We worked all these years
precisely to unfold this way.

IF MOTHER COULD REST

If I rise out of being *her* child,
if I rise out of being *a* child, if
I rise out of my identity, and
drift as a seed before she and my
father called me into the world,
I can see how frightened she's
been of this life. Far away
and out of her reach, I can
wish her peace. At 86, she's
losing her mind. The tragedy
is she didn't lose it sooner.

IF HAWKS COULD SPEAK
OF HEAVEN

On my way home, I pass a stand of oaks
in a field of sheep and lately, in the soft
yellow that flares before dusk, a dozen
hawks or so glide overhead
like darkened kites.

The first few times I slowed to see if
some deer had died or some smaller nest
had been exposed. Nothing but sheep
chewing grass.

They never swoop. Just gather and glide.
Not every day. But here they are today.
This time I pull over, get out, and stare
into their silhouette.

Maybe it's this pocket of wind or well
of light. Or what the tops of
these oaks unveil.

Now two soar higher than the rest.
As if this piece of earth we all drive by
is the one place you never have to land
or look away or swoop. At least for now.
Before the wind no one can see or slow
moves Heaven on.

NOTHING IS SEPARATE

All things are true. The wind through
the Spanish moss tells me that this has
always been. I must keep my heart open
long enough for all things to mix until
the alchemy of Oneness softens my time
on Earth. If you take my hand when I'm
like this, we will know each other in a
way that will never leave us. Dipping
our face in each other's heart, as we
would a stream we come upon deep
in the woods—this makes the tribe
strong. Enough to build something
out of nothing. Enough to love
what-is back into just what it is.

LINEAGE

Old Friends, Old Teachers,
I never meant to crowd you out.
At first I would drop anything
when you would appear. And
then, it was the noise of the world
that made me save you for a more
sacred time. It was obstacle after
obstacle that drew my attention,
while I kept you like a prize for a
quiet simple day. No one told me to
make this separation. I just started
to keep what matters from what
needs to be done. I began a
life of clearing debris in order
to live in the open. But there is
always more debris. And after all
these years you've never failed me;
always waiting in the noise, in
the pain, in the thing
to be cleared.

THE PRACTICE
BEFORE THE PRACTICE

In Japan, before an apprentice can
clay up his hands and work the wheel,
he must watch the master potter for years.
In Hawaii, before a young man can ever
steer a boat, he must sit on the cliff
of his ancestors and simply watch the
sea. In Africa, before the children are
allowed to drum, they must rub the
length of skin stretched over wood
and dream of the animal whose heart
will guide their hands. In Vienna, the
prodigy must visit the piano maker be-
fore ever fingering a scale, to see how
the keys are carved into place. And in
Switzerland, legend has it that before
the watchmaker can couple his tiny
gears, he must sit long enough
to feel the passage of time.

THE APPOINTMENT

What if, on the first sunny day,
on your way to work, a colorful bird
sweeps in front of you down a
street you've never heard of.

You might pause and smile,
a sweet beginning to your day.

Or you might step into that street
and realize there are many ways to work.

You might sense the bird knows some-
thing you don't and wander after.

You might hesitate when the bird
turns down an alley. For now
there is a tension: Is what the
bird knows worth being late?

You might go another block or two,
thinking you can have it both ways.
But soon you arrive at the edge
of all your plans.

The bird circles back for you
and you must decide which
appointment you were
born to keep.

A Thousand Stories On

*If you want to build a ship, don't herd people together to
collect wood and don't assign them tasks and work but rather,
teach them to long for the endless immensity of the sea.*

ANTOINE DE SAINT-EXUPÉRY

GETTING CLOSER

Go on, the voices say, part the veil.
Not with your hands. Hands will only
tangle the hours like a net. Get closer.
So you can part the veil with your breath.
The world keeps moving in on itself. It's
what it does. Cobwebs. Opinions. Moss.
Worries. Dirt. Leaves. History. Go on. Put
them down and get real close. Open your
mouth and inhale all the way to the begin-
ning, which lives within us, not behind us.
Then wait. When something ordinary starts
to glow, we are even closer. When the light
off the river paints the roots of that old willow
just as you pass, the world is telling you to
stop running. Forget what it means, just
stop running. When the moon makes you
finger the wet grass, the veil is parting.
When the knot you carry is loosened,
the veil is parting. When you can't help
but say yes to all that is waiting, the
veil is parting.

THE EARLY SKY IS DEGAS YELLOW

I love this time of year. The only leaves left are
small silhouettes against the sky. They will go
unnoticed once the world wakes. Yesterday,
while we were driving, George was setting
up sawhorses outside his shop. He was help-
ing us make shelves for your pottery. As we
rolled through Parchment, the sun I so love
flooded the intersection and I couldn't see the
light was red. I started through it. You called out.
I blamed it on the sun. You questioned my sight.
We argued briefly. You wondered if I should be
using a table saw. I bristled at the limitation.
Just then the sun flooded you. And for a
moment, I was able to drop my stubborn
denial that things are slowly breaking down.
For the moment, I could drop out of me and
see how hard it is for you who cares so much
for everything you love. I know saying I'll be
careful doesn't always help. As we turned
off Riverview, I felt how much you love me.
So much goes unnoticed once the world
wakes. We are small silhouettes against
the early sky. I love this time of year.

THE PURPOSE OF FISHING

It's hard to say. We gather the rod and
bait and clean the lure, the way we get
degrees. Then cast our line the way we
cast ambition. Then we wait. Until we
think it's all for nothing. If lucky, we
outlast the glare of failure. Once we
stop counting, it seems just being there,
rocking in the stillness, is the catch. And
once we stop waiting, we can hear the beat
of the bottom below the gusts of wind. Then,
and only then, might some big, shiny, arm-
less thing break surface. But the lightweight
rod is sleeping out of reach. So we grab for
what moves in the deep with our hands.
All this to get us wet in a baptism
no one can name.

OVERLOOK

The best thing about heartache,
if I can stand it, is that it makes me
break through the canopy of mind into
a clearing that takes my breath away.
Like now. And all that's gone by
and all that is to come offers
its vastness.

Like a small bird suddenly between
mountains, my heart, having pumped
through obstacles for so long, is stunned.
From here, I could close my eyes and
splinter into slivers of light that would
fill the lungs of everyone I ever loved.

But Mira is sleeping on my feet,
the weight of her innocence begging
me to stay, and the snow is crying
softly, and the thought of never
seeing you laugh makes me return
to the ground, to the ache,
to the days to be lived.

TO BE AND BELONG

Let go your want for greatness
and feel the tool that's in your hand.

Let go your fear of emptiness
and receive the wave still reaching
from the beginning.

It only wants to enliven you
the way water refreshes every hole.

So let the web of things
entangle you.

Only stars are free
and they are so lonely.

Curse what you will
but give thanks

that everything alive
wants something from you.

LOST SPEECH

The more that falls away,
the more knit I am to things
before they speak, drawn into
the waters of silence. When I
listen carefully, I'm pulled be-
low the words of those speaking,
into the current using them, as the
wind uses a reed to get animals to
stop chewing and widen their
eyes. I once followed sunset
into a purple marsh and
stepping on a fallen log,
the tangled brush tugged
the trees to sway. Hundreds
of cranes lifted and I was un-
done. I am now devoted to
the lost step that brings
us into the open.

CHANT

What we want and
what we're given often
serve two different Gods.

How we respond
to their meeting
determines our
path.

THE LONG FIRE

After all this time, you want
me to let you back in. But I've
cleared the ash and broken glass.
I waited till spring to pour a new
foundation. It took almost two
years but it's rebuilt. I'm rebuilt.
Now you want to talk, to resume,
to tell me you didn't know, or you
didn't mean it, or you had no choice.
But that's the point, the ugly stone-
like point. Faced with a choice, you
set the match, or brought the match,
or watched, pretending we didn't
know each other the way we did.
You looked the other way. Even
then, you never called to see if I
made it or how badly I was hurt.
There's no regret in your voice,
only loneliness and a surprise
that the fire, so long put out,
has now reached you.

UNDERSTORY

—The sun has its story
that no curtain can stop.

I've been watching stars
rely on the darkness they
resist. Watching fish struggle
with and against the current.
And hawks glide faster when
their wings don't move.

Still I keep retelling what
happens till it comes out
the way I want.

We try so hard to be the
main character when it's
our point of view that
keeps us from the truth.

The only way to listen to
what can never be said is to
quiet our need to steer the plot.

When jarred by life, we might
unravel the story we tell ourselves
and discover the story we are in,
the one that keeps telling us.

THE FOURTH ORCHID

In a moment of weariness with
who he has become, a sex trader
tells the six frightened girls cornered
in the back of a laundry that he will
let one go. They pull hairs and the
longest is left behind. That night,
on her father's small farm, a little
worm carrying blight tires and lands
on the elm, sparing the willow. The
next season, a sudden gust through
the willow pushes the bee to the next
flower, which given the chance becomes
an orchid that an aging artist talks to
rather than paints. His students think
him mad, except the one who will show
us the inside of beauty. He stays on and
his teacher says in their fourth talk with
the orchid, "I've done away with brushes
and paints." And the spring after the teach-
er dies, the girl with the longest hair, much
quieter than most, seems an orchid her-
self, when the younger artist, so busy with
his paints, sees her reading near a pond.
They will learn each other's histories, but
all depends on the tiredness that makes him
stop and the wind that lifts her face so they
might see each other in this long moment
of complete rendering. In time, they will
build their raft of love and set out
on the soft, relentless sea.

239

FOLLOWING WHISPERS

In Bali, every door is built with a step
to cross because demons can't step, and
every path bends or curves because demons
can only see straight. Tourists check their
e-mail and think this superstitious. Until they
see the Komodo dragons, the largest lizards
on Earth. Once they go after what they think
will fill their hunger, they won't stop until
they die. They get more attention. It all
seems odd till, walking the black sand at
dusk, I feel the breath of the Komodo in
a dark corner of my mind. It's my demon,
leathery, half-deaf, unable to follow whispers.
Surely you have yours. Lately I have trouble
with steps. I can only see straight. And stop-
ping halfway round the world, I feel pushed
by the one hunger; going after what I want
or think I need, not stopping till I die. But
today, I wander into a water temple where
an old man offers a prayer skirt which is
beautiful but confining enough to force
small steps. When I ask for one that fits,
the old man smiles, "It fits just right."
We all line up after chasing the hunger
for thousands of miles, wading through
the water, to put our heads under
the fountain, praying the demon
will be lulled back to sleep.

BREVITY

When someone says, "Get to the point,"
I stop talking. It was Mumon in China in
the summer of 1228 who said, "to test real
gold you must see it through fire." So we
must walk what matters through fire. And
there is no brevity in what we learn from
fire. Or in retrieving what is worth sharing.
Or in what we bring up from the deep like
the pearl diver who painfully tells of the
shell that cut his hand as he scooped the
pearl and how his blood blossomed
underwater like a red net he keeps
dreaming of.

Life meanders to insure we are listen-
ing. Take the birder I meet who tells me
of the blackpoll warbler who weighs as
much as a ball point pen, who migrates
every year from Nova Scotia to Venezuela,
pumping its tiny wings for 90 hours without
rest, without food, without touching down,
because the water will cause its wings to sleep
and it will die. The point, to keep winging.

The thrill of the birder makes me go home
and sit very still for a long time till the finch
I know thinks I'm a pole. I open my palm and
wait. It takes forty minutes but she hops into
my hand. I am stunned. She feels like a warm

breeze. I can feel her tiny heart, so fast it stops
my mind. She is soft and uncontainable. My
own heart starts to beat faster. Both of us—
so soft, so necessary, beyond any point.
She flies from my hand as she must—
leaving me bereft of all knowing,
just slightly aglow.

PATHWAYS

I don't know why I was born
with this belief in something
deeper and larger than we can
see. It's always called. Even as
a boy, I knew that trees and light
and sky all point to some timeless
center out of view. I've spent my
life listening to that center and filter-
ing it through my heart. This listening
and filtering is how I hear the music of
all souls. After sixty years, I've run out
of ways to name it. Even now, my heart
won't stop transforming. In a moment
of seeing, it takes the shape of my eye.
In a moment of speaking, the shape
of my tongue. In a moment of silence,
it slips back into the lake of center.
When you kiss me, it takes the shape
of your lip. When our dog sleeps with
us, it takes the shape of her curl. When
the hummingbird feeds her babies, it
takes the shape of her beak carefully
dropping food into our throats.

HOW WE
TALKED

I knew him well,
though not in words.
We'd take long walks.
And animals unsure of
us would step on leaves,
gone before we'd turn.

He'd say, what matters
is like that.

But love, I'd say, is like
water rising and fire
spreading.

He'd never disagree,
just go silent.

I was with him the day
he died. The light was
still asleep.

And seeing dawn
before the rest of us,
he raised his head
one final time.

"Look everywhere . . ."
he said. And he was
gone before I turned.

244

THE EMPTY NECKLACE

We each have one, made of the bare
moments we stumble into, when
everything is still and complete.

I'm thinking of the long silence months
ago after we admitted how much
we need each other.

Or the time in winter when the snowy
pines were creaking and swaying a
hundred feet up like the eye of the
Earth opening slightly.

Or the time in early fall when you
were pinching a pot in the sun
and our dog was chewing on a stick
and I started to cry.

And the moment I woke from surgery
too soon and my soul had to decide
which way to swim.

Sometimes, when the wind sweeps
the next task from my mind, I am
returned to the moment before I
was born: floating with a brief sense
of all there is, just as I was ushered
into the world with our need to
find that feeling between us.

OH GRANDMA

I'm telling your story again,
this time in San Francisco. I feel
you very near, in my throat, behind
my eyes, so much that I'm pulled
from the room into the scene I so
remember. It's always the same.
I'm eight, on your basement steps,
but this time I speak as I am now.
You're holding my hands.
We're in between worlds.

You ask if I've seen your
husband, Nehemiah. I rub
your hands and promise
to look for him.

Oh Grandma, you've been gone
for twenty years. You lift my chin
and smile. I'm overcome. You have
no idea. I think I learned all
I need to know from you
on these stairs.

Your smile smells like potato
pancakes. You don't say anything.
You just cup my face and
I break into a flower
aching with certainty.

You get up slowly and waddle
up the stairs. I'm thrown heart-years
forward back to the group. It's hard
to say anything. Finally, I shrug.

Oh Grandma, in the Brooklyn
I go to when feeling lost, there
you are, leaning from your kitchen
into the brick alley, except
the alley is my heart.

And the light behind you
is where we come from
and where we're all going.

19TH AND IRVING

I wake this morning with a sadness.
Can't find it. Can't shake it. But with
my third coffee, I notice the French doors
on the balcony across the street, slightly open.
They seem to speak in a language no one hears
unless sad. Suddenly, the whole world depends
on the thin opening of these doors: on what
they let in, on what they let out. Like my mind,
or your heart. All day I look for opened doors:
left open, blown open, broken open. Doors
whose latches have finally worn down. Is this
what sadness is for: to wear our latches down?

DISAPPEARING

What do I tell everyone
who's been waiting? That
I've turned into a bird? That
I can only follow light and
wind? That only when you
need me, can I turn back
into a person with arms that
hold and legs that fetch?

I can't explain. There are
days I am torn like a flag
and nights where I spread
like frost across your pane.

This is only disappointing
to those who were count-
ing on me to get larger.

LIGHT MEETING LIGHT

As I went quiet, a cloud parted
in my mind and the light within
made it briefly to the page.

I rubbed my eyes
to search what had surfaced,
the way a diver catches his
breath and wipes the muck
from his mask.

Just as I began to under-
stand, the sun came
through the maple,
covering the page.

When I looked,
a cardinal was bobbing
out my window, as if
to say, keep trying.

THE POEMS

When starting out, I was so excited
that anything showed up, I thought
I was done. But somewhere along
the way, I realized they are alive
and I wasn't wrestling them into
view. They, respecting my effort,
agreed to be seen. Not to be re-
vealed, but to be loved. Now I
circle back in the morning to see
what they need from me. Just more
of my attention which starts with me
undressing what I know. For the
longest time I thought I was revising.
It's more a conversation in which I
keep learning how to listen. And
when I do, they will after a time
pull aside a cloth or cloud to make
obvious the reason they have come.

SIDE BY SIDE

Until we trip, we don't understand
why it takes so long to get up. Until
we lose our way, we have no patience
for indecision. Eventually, we land
so close to the shallow breathing of
another that it doesn't matter where
we're from or where we're going, if
we're living like a waterfall or asleep
with our eyes open. The only thing
that matters is the hand we offer and
the assurance that everything will be
alright, though we really don't know.

THE ANGEL OF GRIEF

Loss plays us like a violin, never free
of its rub. It simply lessens its intensity
till only the one closest to what was lost
can hear it. If you haven't lost something
or someone, this will seem sad, even fright-
ening. But after a century of heart-time, I
went to the immortals who envy us our
ability to feel and forget. They looked
at me with their longing to be human.
And the saddest among them took my
hand and said, *"I would give Eternity to
live with what you're given, and to feel
what is opened by what is taken away."*

LOSING YOURSELF

We're having lunch at the harbor,
salads and tea, and Bob starts talking
about losing himself in certain pieces
of music. Not losing track of time. Or
forgetting to meet me in half an hour.
More that who he is pools, for the mo-
ment, in a larger sea. He says it's scary,
'cause he's not sure he'll come back
as himself. But being drawn out this
way makes him feel alive. Now Susan
talks about the small woodpecker who
flew into our window during the week.
How she found it in the flowers, fright-
ened but alert. How she tried to help it
fly. How she pinched its little legs and
nothing. It had broken its toothpick of a
back. She put it in a towel, in a shoebox.
When I came home, I saw her holding
the little thing, its soft eyes flitting. It
was drinking drops of water from her
finger. I will never forget that drinking.
The next day the little one died. Susan
says she won't be the same. We peck at
our salads and drink our tea. The light
spills between us. The three of us
drinking from each other's fingers.

Skip's Poem

Two deer, fur
thickening for winter,
nibble at the pines.

The taller tugs at some
needles and the branch
drops snow on its face.
It looks old and wise.
Were it that easy.

Yet this is how it
happens. Though the
drop of wisdom on our
face can take years.

The smaller deer
licks snow from the
larger one's ear.

This is how wisdom
is passed: drop of
snow, lick of ear.

This too can
take years.

A THOUSAND STORIES ON

We play with the dog on the floor
and laugh and lean into each other
and your eyes which I know so well
stop me. We talk some more, taking
off the day before our clothes. Holding
you lightly as the wind dies down makes
me believe that intimacy is the silk of the
world. The rest of the night is one long
kiss, as is this life. In a while you will
sleep. Tomorrow, the sun will curl up
the mailbox and skip to the top of the
maple. Like two cut flowers adrift in
the sea, how did we find each other?

INCANDESCENCE

I have worked months
on lines like these.
But I am not these lines nor
the effort to shape them.

Now that I have written books
I find I am not a book.
Now that I have sung
bouquets of song, I confess
I am not the song.

Now that I have loved,
I discover that what I am
shows itself to be touched
but is not the touch.

Even when feeling the wind
blow aside the veils
I cling to,

even when loving
the instant of seeing,
I am not what is sighted
nor the instant it is seen.

Undressed of all there is to do,
I vanish in a gesture
that is everywhere.

The End of All Striving

Life isn't something you possess.
It's something you take part in and witness.

LOUIS C. K.

THE RING OF RINGS

As a broken door lets in the light,
a broken heart lets in the world.

No one likes this,
but we can't grow without it.

And no matter how we try,
we can't hold on to everything.

For the mind is a net
and all nets have holes.

But you mustn't worry,
because the heart is a sponge.

Still, it's easier to fall in love
than to stay in love.

Easier to have a dream
than to live a dream.

In this, we're all apprentices,
who always begin again.

I Promise You

I was in a circle of those who
climbed from the sea of trouble
onto the shore of a day like today.
We were tired, aglow, broken.

Out of a sudden silence
a young woman stood and sang
You've Got a Friend. When I heard,
"You just call out my name and
I'll be there . . ." I saw you all.

No vow has meant more to me.
Yet there was the time I couldn't
get there. And the time I was afraid
to come for some dark reason too
familiar for me to understand.

I am sorry for the wounds my
absence has caused.

We try like birds awakened by
a tone of light to fly into each
other's need. And always
wind throws us off.

I am so sorry not to be
what I promised.

But like a whale whose tears
only add to the ocean that slows
him down, I swim to you.
I swim to you.

THE BETTER WAY TO GO

One at a time, they come off the plane:
looking for someone, or arriving alone,
returning, or beginning. As they get off,
I wait to get on. Suddenly, it's not
just the 11:35 to Chicago. Now we're
immigrants leaving Europe. Or the
thousands filing in and out to see the
lost Buddhas of Cambodia. Or the box-
cars with no exit. They get off. I wait to
get on. It doesn't matter where we're go-
ing. I want to stop the old man shuffling.
He seems to carry a secret. It weighs him
down. It makes him search the floor for
the crack to the underworld he was told
would be here. We keep coming and going.
Born. Dying. In and out of life. Only no
one knows whether getting on or getting
off is the better way to go. The old man
pushes through. He's looking for his bag-
gage. Here's another with a limp in her
heart. It makes me want to stand and
hum the one true thing I know. And
what if I could sing it till it undresses
all our cries? Would anyone recognize
it, know it as their own? Would some
join in? I'm asked to board. To get on
with it. She looks at my passport to see
if it's me. As if to say, *Are you you?*
I think she understands.

THE WHALES OF AUSTRALIA

Every year pilot whales swim in pods through
the Bass Strait which separates the isle of Tasmania
and Southern Australia. They repeat this journey
with a passion to reach the polar waters.

Yesterday, sixty-four long-finned pilots stranded
themselves on a stretch of Anthony's beach.

The sight of these mountainous fish—the ocean
pooling along their slick, heavy sides—even
stopped the tourists who stop for no one.

Within an hour, fifty volunteers were pulling
slings beneath their soft bellies; trying to
drag them back into the sea. Some spent the
night pouring water on their ancient faces.

They saved eleven. What made these whales
strand themselves? What made strangers rub
water on their improbable backs?

It is as much our destiny to swim with
no end as it is to get stuck; as it is to
return each other to the deep.

INSIDE OUT

I was taken aback, when
joining a fitness club, at
the history of my body: a
rib removed, torn ligaments
in an ankle, torn muscle in a
knee, torn meniscus in the
other, arthritic thumbs, a
skull bone worn thin
by a tumor.

At first, I felt battered,
but smiled to realize that
I stand like a small cliff
worn full of holes in which
stray birds nest and I wake
with the dreams they have
while resting in me.

Each question carried
for a lifetime opens
like a hole worn in stone
through which the wind
finally sings.

STALLED BETWEEN DREAMS

I'm standing on Macdougal near Bleecker
where the heat of the living swarms on by.
I can feel everyone's anticipation and dis-
appointment, the eagerness not to miss
anything and the windedness at getting
there too late. And stalled between dreams,
a few like me stare out, surprised that nothing
is lacking. Now someone steps in a puddle that
splashes up my knee. It's a baptism of sorts, an
anonymous blessing that says there's nowhere
to go. I inhale the dust of all our attempts to
love which makes me cough. And there you
have it. Now my dream-dust is up for grabs.
Yeats pined for Byzantium and the Vikings
longed for Valhalla. But I through chance
and tumble have found a dirty corner of
Heaven right here. A sad angel in a torn
shirt asks me for a dime. It's God again
in one of his infinite disguises.

MEETING MY SELVES

I came upon a younger me. He was
pushing against everything. Seeing what
would hold and what would give way. What
gave way he thought weaker. What resisted
he thought oppressive. I was embarrassed at
how little I knew. Then I stumbled on an artist
obsessed with the fire of creation. He thought
it a sacred obligation. He threw everything into
the flames. Those close thought him an arsonist.
I felt guilty for those I burned against their will.
Midway I found a fish-like man whose chest
was pried open like a ragged shell. This was
me tossed ashore by cancer. I felt grateful for
the cracking of my stubbornness with time
enough to be. Along the way I dreamt of an
old holy man. I can't say he was me but I have
met him many times. He stays in the world
though he faces the interior. Whatever the
difficulty, he stops to bless whatever is near.
When I was near death, he stopped to bless
me. I have searched for him ever since. When
I close my fear, I feel his hands entering my
hands. When I close my worry, I feel his
eyes parting the curtain of my eyes.

FINDING OUR WAY

He dropped the phone. The man
who first brought me to the sea,
though he couldn't hear what the
sea said to me. The father who locked
the door when the bully bloodied me
on our back steps. The one who cried
when I had cancer, though he wouldn't
come when I was sick from chemo. The
Depression-era boy in a man's body who
dreams of sailing his way out of trouble.
The father I haven't seen in 15 years, who
won't die in my heart, the 90-year-old
whose spine is calcifying, whose speech
is slowing. The one worn to a gentleness
that makes me want to hold him. I said,
"I'd like to see you one more time."
He dropped the phone and began
to weep. I don't know what we're
doing or where we are, but I've
waited my whole life to be here.

THERE

Whenever I try to say what matters,
what matters pulls back, slips out of
view. But it is there. I felt it in the
Jewish Cemetery in Prague, between
the wet leaf and the broken stone.
There, in the still breathing of the
painted mime in Barcelona. In the
jaw of Table Mountain overlooking
Cape Town. In the shadowy trees
lacing the face of Paris. There, in
the quiver of our mouths when we
make love. And in John's last smile
as he stared out the window at some-
thing we couldn't see. I see it in the
tongue of my father now that he can't
speak. It waits in the center of clouds
and escapes as rain. I've tried so hard
to drink from it. When I think I've
touched it, it leaves. And I drift.
Until great loss or sudden wonder
sweeps me to my knees. When
I give up, it lifts my face.

Rethinking Time

You can't hoard moments like coins.
You can only enter them.

You can't trim hours like wood or glass.
You can only bathe in them.

You can't add days like a drop of God
to every godless drink.

You can only immerse yourself
in the river that won't stop carrying us.

Begrudge time and it will skip over you.
But enter, bathe, kiss, and bow. Immerse
yourself in the time you have and time
will carry you through the eye
of its needle into all that is.

LESSON PLAN

The lost bird remembers how to sing
as it splashes in a puddle
and forgets how to fly.

This was the teacher's answer
to his student's complaints
about living on Earth.

FOR HIS STUDENTS
(FOR STEVE SEVERIN)

I have come to tell you that your teacher
is gone. Much too soon. He was a good
man with a good heart and he was my friend.
Everything else grows like a branch from this
strong wood. He was a great teacher because
he loved you. Because he believed you are
young horses who more than crossing the
stream can drink from it. He would hold
up a question like a lantern, swing it ahead
and shout, "What do you see?" Then hurry
you into your future, barking, "Go! Bring
back what you see!"

So how do you love a teacher who's died?
You keep swinging questions like lanterns
in the dark. You tell the story of how he
surprised your mind into opening. You
keep the part of your soul that he intro-
duced to you awake. You challenge some-
one younger than you to care. You keep
his tradition of always saying thank you.

He was my friend. I loved him and I loved
how he never stopped looking for the roots
of life; though he was more about looking
than finding. Our friend is gone. Much
too soon. His name was Steve. When he
talked about you, his heart was in his eyes.

HOLDING WIDE

We were in the car doing errands,
zipping down Tenth, when Susan
blurted, "Turn Around! Turn Around!"
I pulled off, on the shoulder, the car
bumping over gravel, waiting for an
opening, looking both ways, "What
is it? What is it?" I thought something
was wrong. "No. No. Just turn around!
There! On that pole! Keep going! Slow
Down! Watch! There's a car behind you!"

On the pole, a turkey vulture sunning
itself, wings spread, six or seven feet,
chest up, head tipping east then west;
as if it were carrying the eye of
God. We pulled off under an old
maple, cars like us whizzing by.

The great bird held, ten minutes and
counting. We watched as our weekend
others kept shaking us with their speed.
We couldn't speak. The great eye
seemed to look at us, as if to say,
"You have seen. What now?"

I took Susan's hand.
We drove away slowly.
The great bird was holding wide.

There was no one to tell. But that
night I dreamt that the bird was my
soul, waiting for me to build my pole
to nowhere, so it could land and inspire
me from the labor of my maze.

THE DEEPER SONG

Years ago I wrote a song on the piano,
discovered its patterns, played it over
and over, so I could remember. Even
tried to score it. When we moved, I
found a good spot for the upright, had
her tuned, but seldom got to play. There
was the tree that almost fell on the house
and your mother's surgery and the new push
at work. Sometimes I'd pause near the keys
before bed, feeling their tug, but I was so
tired and I couldn't find the song. Then
my father turned 90 and I went to see him.
And I had that awful spell with my stomach.
Then I lost my job. Finally, when you were
out and the dog was asleep and the sun was
almost down, I dusted her off, afraid I'd for-
gotten everything. But after a few wrong
notes my hands took over, as if to say,
"We've been waiting." And the song
beyond its opening led me to a run of
notes that fingered the spot in my heart
that carried me through everything. As
if the song I thought I'd written was
just a pouch in which the deeper
song had been waiting.

ENDLESS POOLS

I am awake. It wasn't always so.
It may not last for long. So let me
say this while my heart is beating like
a river. This life is more than we can
bear. It's taken years to learn this, to
feel this, to know this in my bones. I'm
not talking about giving up or enduring.
I mean we're not designed to bear it all.
Anymore than the sun bears the sky or
the wind bears the thousands of leaves
it moves through. We're only meant to
let things through. I am awake. This time
I fell to it. I was productive. Some said on
fire. Then I tripped on something small.
Like a pebble in your shoe. And fell out
of the dance I had created. The one by
which I knew my worth. I couldn't get
it back. It depressed me for months. But
like a whale I kept diving down and com-
ing up. Despite the parting of my dream.
Now I'm awake as I never imagined. This
doesn't preclude pain or weather or dis-
appointment. These as well as joy land
in a lake-like depth that has held us since
birth. Come. Look. Like an endless pool
that clears after a violent rain, you can
see through me. I am awake.

THE SILENT WE

Through the hotel wall a woman cries,
"I can't do this anymore!" One soft life
in one small box in thirty-story boxes
across the city. She sends her alarm like
a cell letting the body know it can't hold
up its part. If I were a superhero, I'd put
my hand to the wall between us and with
my X-ray vision, I'd search her heart like a
surgeon of love, pouring light from my palm
through all the walls so they could disappear
for one long moment, enough for her to heal
herself. For I have slumped against my own
walls, unable to continue. But I am only me.
And so I put my hand to the wall between
us and draw as much of her suffering as I
can, the way a shaman would suck venom
from a snakebite and spit it in the grass.

WE AS BLIND SCULPTORS

—to consider everything, profess nothing.

I have sought like a child of pain
a place where it might stop
and of course,
of way upon way,
of so much pushing through the dark
to flower and never be let alone
by all the flying things
dying for sweetness,
it never stops.

And all I've felt has risen
like noise into music into echo
till everything has settled
and I've begun to speak from
a clearing that neither opens
or closes.

Now it makes no sense
to expect other than to breathe,
one inhalation after another,
and to love, one drawing in
after the next,
till loves merge
into a non-expectant life,
into a wind
that makes us want
to climb from the rest,

to see the rest,
to feel the rest
in having been lifted,
even briefly.

On this walking island
you call my solitude,
the winds are all one could imagine,
enough to undress
a god of its mystery
or a human aspect
of its importance,
enough to play the flute of bone
that makes pain a sensation
and love, a sense of rising.

Rising Through Our Faults

I was hiking near the tree line when it started to
rain and I was washed of where to go. Looking about,
I realized that the fates wait for the moment that we
finalize our plans to set our maps on fire. They send
a storm to blow the secret from our hand. And let a
downpour wash the trail from under our feet. Not
to be harsh but to force us to believe in ourselves.
When overcome with things too big to understand,
our mind will stretch. When stopped by things too
delicate to hold, our grip will soften. And touched
by things impossible to name, we drop all pretense.
I was caught in the rain, in between worlds, and I
could see: What makes these mountains majestic is
how they were ripped from the earth and frozen into
place. To stand before them dwarfs all human trouble.
It's the same when our souls are caught rising through
our faults. When forced into the open, we break
into majesty and settle in our place.

WHERE TO NOW?

Now that I've come out of hiding,
my fears are forgetting to be afraid.

Now that I've dropped my opinions
in the rain, my story is too small
to cover my heart.

Now that I've put down what I thought
was important, I'm surprised by angels
lost along the way.

How we got here doesn't matter
and where we're going is just
something for the mind to chew.

I'll meet you here, in the palace
that difficulty opens—the magical
doorway, the shape of who we are.

Falling Open

I couldn't keep the damn glasses
clean. Kept wiping them and cursing
them. And my left ear was getting worse.
Those across the room were shouting
secrets behind a waterfall. But I kept
going. Kept wiping the damn glasses.
Kept trying to make sense of what I
couldn't hear. Then after the cocoon
my soul was eating through gave way,
I arrived in this newness I can't explain.
I realized it was my eyes, not the glasses.
And the waterfall was in my head. When
the optometrist flipped her lenses in the
dark, something deep inside let go. When
she reached the one through which I could
see, the tumblers in the lock that is me fell
open. When the kind audiologist tucked
the hearing aid in my ear, the waterfall
ceased. I left like a child, hearing birds
again. Like the Wizard of Oz, we
become smaller and softer when
our curtain is pulled.

THE END OF ALL STRIVING

In the moment of reading in public,
I coax the bird in my chest to wake
and fly above the audience. And
finding no way out, he returns
to tuck his wings and perch
above my heart.

I often wait till everyone has left;
to see if the emptiness was
happy with my offering.

This time, the man who cleans up
shuffles in. After stacking the chairs,
he puts out his hand, "I saw a lot
of your books in the basement."

We shake. He adds, "I haven't
read any." I'm quick to say,
"That's alright."

We sit on a table for a while.
I ask, "Why'd you want to meet?"
He shrugs, "My friend told me
you have a nice smile."

BEING CARRIED

The things that happen to us
are trying to have a conversation,
to make us stop or turn around.

The things that matter are waiting
for us to drop down after the first
conversation has relaxed our will.

Then they will shine their light
without warning, like a doctor,
into the back of our eyes and ask,
"How long have you avoided rest?"

If we answer truthfully, they will
introduce us to beauty who after
a time will make us cry and throw
our judgments into the sea.

My Favorite Glass

You broke my favorite glass.
Now you feel bad. It was my
favorite because I touched it
so many times. I looked at its
pieces you so carefully gathered.
I think it was tired and wanted
to go. I held the largest shard
and it glittered. I held it to my
ear and it said, "I am now free."
What makes things special is
who brings them and what
they carry. You are special.
Our dog is special. The wind
through the tops of the trees
before dawn which you were
amazed by before you broke
the glass is special. So don't
feel bad. Just feel.

BEAUTY IS EVERYWHERE

The old Asian man is playing one
string so completely that the hymns of
the Universe part the air, making me stop,
unsure where I'm going. He's surrounded
by dollar bills and petals, each a currency
we can't do without. It's giving ourselves
to one small thing that makes beauty come
out of hiding. Like when you led the baby
robin from our garage and it hovered once
free, as if to thank you. Today I feel like
an old string plucked by what endures.
It makes me quiver. The tulips are so
bright. Or is it that I finally see them?

BE A CIRCLE

I wish you the ability to breathe
after pain, to begin again, though
nothing else seems possible.

I wish you resilience: to part like
the ocean and accept like the sky.

I wish you survival: to take in life
like a trapped miner finding an
airhole and praising it as God.

I wish you courage: to ask of
everything you meet, "What
bridge are we?"

I wish that the kindness-that-you-
are can brighten your way,
like orange leaves falling
about the face of a doe.

I wish you endless journey
that seldom appears
as we imagine.

I wish you curiosity: to make
a boat of wonder and an
oar of gratitude.

SEEING IT THROUGH

To see it and walk through it
when it opens is everything. It's
how Picasso discovered cubism.
How Miles Davis stumbled onto
Dolphin Street. How Derek Jeter
knew the relay would land between
first base and home and no one else
would be there. It's through this
opening that Albert Schweitzer
saw his hospital in Africa long
before he was a doctor. It's here
that we all see love waiting in its
open field, though there are storms
all around. It's what a whale goes
for each time it breaches. It's
how I find the poems. It's how
the kind know how to help.

THE HARD HUMAN SPRING

We each arrive with a gift hidden in
a wound and many years to birth it, each
given a heat to carry and rough seas to calm
it, each seeded with a worthiness and love after
love through which to accept it, each called to
enter sorrow like an underwater cave with the
breathless chance to break surface in the same
world with everything aglow. If we make it this
far, we can, on any given day, marvel that clouds
are clouds and name ourselves. We can use the
gift born of our wound to find an unmarked spot
from which to live. If we settle there, giving our
all without giving ourselves away, the heart
within our heart will flower and the whole
world will eat of its nectar.

The Moment of Poetry

When the sweet ache of being alive,
lodged between who you are
and who you will be,
is awakened,
befriend this moment.
It will guide you.
Its sweetness is what holds you.
Its ache is what moves you on.

The Way
Under the Way

For all that has been written,
for all that has been read, we
are led to this instant where one
of us will speak and one of us will
listen, as if no one has ever placed
an oar into that water.

It doesn't matter how we come
to this. We may jump to it or be
worn to it. Because of great pain.
Or a sudden raw feeling that this
is all very real. It may happen in a
parking lot when we break the eggs
in the rain. Or watching each other
in our grief.

But here we will come. With very
little left in the way.

When we meet like this, I may not
have the words, so let me say it now:
Nothing compares to the sensation
of being alive in the company of
another. It is God breathing on
the embers of our soul.

GRATITUDES

Much of a poet's life is spent hunting out glimpses of a Source too big for words, and nothing else seems worth sharing. And so, my gratitude to those who've loved me with their patience, especially when things were slow in making sense. Deep gratitude to Bread for the Journey, a tribe of givers scattered across North America. Their simple devotion to giving, person to person, is an inoculation against the strain of greed that grows within our culture. And how can I thank Wayne Muller, Marianna Cacciatore, and Brandy Sacks for the generosity of their belief and encouragement through the years. And to my agent, Jennifer Rudolph Walsh, for her fierce care and thoughtful guidance, as well as Eve Attermann, Raffaella De Angelis, and the rest of the WME team for their committed excellence. To Bill Clegg for his early support of these poems. And to Brooke Warner for her steadfast friendship. And to my publicist, Eileen Duhne, for her kindness and loyalty. I'm also deeply grateful for the love of the Sounds True family: to Tami Simon for her strength of heart, and to my editor, Haven Iverson, and my producer, Steve Lessard, for their care and commitment to the depth of the journey.

It's impossible to inhabit wonder or to find the way under the way without friends. So deep gratitude to my dear friends for sharing their wonder and their trouble. Especially George, Don, Paul, Skip, TC, David, Kurt, Pam, Patti, Karen, Paula, Ellen, Linda, Michelle, Rich, Carolyn, Henk, Sandra, Elesa, and Sally. And to my brother Howard for his unshakeable care. And to Oprah Winfrey for her braid of truth and love.

And to my compadre, Paul Bowler, who always looks for what matters in everyone. And to my old friend of the long journey, Robert Mason, I owe so much to what opens when we're together. And to my wife, Susan, who loves me when I put all I know and don't know down. Your heart is a great teacher. Finally, to my reader, you are always alone and never alone. As am I. May these poems be threads by which we find each other.

NOTES

IN CONVERSATION WITH LIFE

xv *"For me, the poems arrive . . . you own feeling."* This paragraph first appeared in the preface to my book *Inside the Miracle: Enduring Suffering, Approaching Wholeness* (Boulder, CO: Sounds True, 2015), xx–xxi.

BOOK ONE: SUITE FOR THE LIVING

5 *Breaking Surface, section page, epigraph:* from *Selected Poems, Pablo Neruda,* edited by Nathaniel Tarn (New York: Dell Publishing, 1972), 275.

49 *Fire in the Temple:* This poem appears in a chapter with the same title that traces the discovery of the poem in my book *The One Life We're Given: Finding the Wisdom That Waits in Your Heart* (New York: Atria, 2016), 209.

70 *An Open Hand:* An earlier version of this poem appears in my book *The Endless Practice: Becoming Who You Were Born to Be,* (New York: Atria, 2015), 124.

71 *Least Complicated, epigraph:* An Ojibway saying, from *The Traveler's Journal,* edited by Lim and Sam Shapiro (Bali: Half Angel Press, 2007), 63.

87 *Suite for the Living, section page, epigraph:* Dogen, cited in *Practice of the Wild,* Gary Snyder (Berkeley: Counterpoint, 1990), 27.

88 *Endgame:* This poem also appears in the expanded edition of my book *Inside the Miracle* (Boulder, CO: Sounds True, 2015). The poem first appeared in the original edition of *Inside the Miracle,* then titled *Acre of Light* (Ithaca House Books, 1994) and again in the original edition of *Suite for the Living* (Bread for the Journey International, 2004).

BOOK TWO: INHABITING WONDER

99 *The Keepers of Kindness, section page, epigraph:* from *George Seferis: A Poet's Journal, 1945–1951,* translated by Athan Anagnostopoulos (Cambridge, MA: Harvard University Press, 1974), 59.

Editions, 1998). Antoine de Saint-Exupéry (1900–1944) was a French writer and aviator, best remembered for his novella *The Little Prince* (*Le Petit Prince*). He was a successful commercial pilot before World War II. He joined the French Air Force at the outbreak of war, flying reconnaissance missions. He disappeared on a reconnaissance flight over the Mediterranean in July 1944. In 1998, east of Riou Island south of Marseille, a fisherman named Jean-Claude Bianco found a silver identity bracelet bearing the names of Saint-Exupéry and of his wife, Consuelo, hooked to a piece of fabric, presumably from his flight suit.

264 *The Whales of Australia:* An earlier prose version of this poem appears in the chapter "Making Our Way" in my book *The One Life We're Given*, 88.

289 *The Hard Human Spring:* An earlier prose version of this poem appears in my book *The Endless Practice*, 195.

PERMISSIONS

T hanks for permission to reprint excerpts from the following previously published works:

Excerpted paragraph in "In Conversation with Life" first appeared in the preface to my book *Inside the Miracle* (Boulder, CO: Sounds True, 2015), xx–xxi.

SUITE FOR THE LIVING

Excerpt from *Selected Poems, Pablo Neruda,* edited by Nathaniel Tarn (New York: Dell Publishing, 1972), 275.

An earlier version of "Fire in the Temple" appears in my book *The One Life We're Given* (New York: Atria, 2016), 209.

Ojibway saying, from *The Traveler's Journal,* edited by Lim and Sam Shapiro (Bali: Half Angel Press, 2007), 63.

A prose version of "Gemseed" appears as the story "In the Mirror" in my book *As Far As the Heart Can See* (Deerfield Beach, FL: HCI Communications, 2011), 95.

"Endgame," which also appears in the expanded edition of my book *Inside the Miracle* (Boulder, CO: Sounds True, 2015). The poem first appeared in the original edition of *Inside the Miracle,* then titled *Acre of Light* (Ithaca House Books, 1994) and again in the original edition of *Suite for the Living* (Bread for the Journey International, 2004).

Apple Farm Poetry Reader (Three Rivers, MI): "Practicing," "Utterance-That-Rises-Briefly-from-the-Source."

Essential Sufism (HarperSanFrancisco): "Freefall," "God's Wounds," "Practicing."

Greenfield Review Press, from *Acre of Light:* "Endgame."

New Hampshire College Journal: "On the Way to Coney Island."

Prayers for Healing (Conari Press): "Freefall," "God's Wounds."

Sufi, A Journal of Sufism (London): "Before the Twice-Locked Gates," "Fighting the Instrument," "Freefall," "God's Wounds," "Walking North."

The Patient's Voice: Experiences of Illness (F.A. Davis Co.): "The Music Beneath the Music."

The Texas Observer: "One Step Closer."

The Journal of Pastoral Care and Counseling: "If You Want a True Friend."

The first edition of *Suite for the Living* was published by Bread for the Journey, © 2004 by Mark Nepo.

INHABITING WONDER

"In the Sea of Others," first appeared in the anthology *Wounded Healers,* edited by Rachel Naomi Remen (Mill Valley, CA: Wounded Healers Press, 1994).

Excerpts from Rumi, in *The Soul of Rumi,* translated by Coleman Barks (San Francisco: HarperSanFrancisco, 2001).

The Journal of Pastoral Care and Counseling: "Joining the Circus."

The first edition of *Inhabiting Wonder* was published by Bread for the Journey, © 2004 by Mark Nepo.

THE WAY UNDER THE WAY

An earlier prose version of "The Whales of Australia" appears in my book *The One Life We're Given,* 88.

Excerpt from Kukai, in *The Enlightened Heart,* edited by Stephen Mitchell (New York: Harper & Row, 1989), 36, 159, 163.

Excerpt from *The Little Prince,* Antoine de Saint-Exupery (London: Wordsworth Editions, 1998).

Earlier prose versions of "Below Our Strangeness," "The Practice Before the Practice," and "The Hard Human Spring" appear in my book *The Endless Practice* (New York, Atria, 2015).

"The Appointment" first appeared in the chapter "Beyond Our Awareness" in my book *Seven Thousand Ways to Listen* (New York, Atria, 2012), 9.

"Attendant Spirits," "Incandescence," and "The Way Under the Way" first appeared in the journal *Sufi.*

"Pathways" first appeared in *Parabola,* Volume 36, Number 4, Winter 2011– 12, 13.

"We As Blind Sculptors" first appeared in *2 Plus 2: A Journal Of International Writing,* 1987, Lausanne, Switzerland.

The Journal of Pastoral Care and Counseling: "Stalled Between Dreams," "The Silent We," and "Seeing It Through."

"Inside Out" originally appeared in a slightly different form in the first edition of my book of poems, *Inhabiting Wonder* (Mill Valley, CA: Bread for the Journey, 2004), 44.

About the Author

Mark Nepo moved and inspired readers and seekers all over the world with his number one *New York Times* bestseller *The Book of Awakening*. Beloved as a poet, teacher, and storyteller, Mark has been called "one of the finest spiritual guides of our time," "a consummate storyteller," and "an eloquent spiritual teacher." His work is widely accessible and used by many, and his books have been translated into more than twenty languages. He has published eighteen books and recorded thirteen audio projects. In 2015, he was given a life-achievement award by AgeNation. In 2016, he was named by *Watkins: Mind Body Spirit* as one of the 100 most spiritually influential living people.

Recent work includes *The One Life We're Given* (Atria, 2016), *Inside the Miracle* (Sounds True), selected by *Spirituality & Health Magazine* as one of the Best Ten Books of 2015, *The Endless Practice* (Atria), cited by *Spirituality & Practice* as one of the Best Spiritual Books of 2014, his book of poems, *Reduced to Joy* (Viva Editions), cited by *Spirituality & Practice* as one of the Best Spiritual Books of 2013, a 6 CD box set of teaching conversations based on the poems in *Reduced to Joy* (Sounds True, 2014), and *Seven Thousand Ways to Listen* (Atria), which won the 2012 Books for a Better Life Award.

Mark was part of Oprah Winfrey's *The Life You Want Tour* in 2014 and has appeared several times with Oprah on her *Super Soul Sunday* program on OWN TV. He has also been interviewed by Robin Roberts on *Good Morning America*. *The Exquisite Risk* was cited by *Spirituality & Practice* as one of the Best Spiritual Books of 2005, calling it "one of the best books we've ever read on what it takes to live an authentic life." Mark devotes his writing and teaching to the journey of inner transformation and the life of relationship. He continues to offer readings, lectures, and retreats. Please visit Mark at MarkNepo.com, threeintentions.com, and info@wmeimgspeakers.com.

ABOUT SOUNDS TRUE

Sounds True is a multimedia publisher whose mission is to inspire and support personal transformation and spiritual awakening. Founded in 1985 and located in Boulder, Colorado, we work with many of the leading spiritual teachers, thinkers, healers, and visionary artists of our time. We strive with every title to preserve the essential "living wisdom" of the author or artist. It is our goal to create products that not only provide information to a reader or listener, but that also embody the quality of a wisdom transmission.

For those seeking genuine transformation, Sounds True is your trusted partner. At SoundsTrue.com you will find a wealth of free resources to support your journey, including exclusive weekly audio interviews, free downloads, interactive learning tools, and other special savings on all our titles.

To learn more, please visit SoundsTrue.com/freegifts or call us toll-free at 800.333.9185.

SOUNDS TRUE
many voices, one journey